UPDATED ZANZIBAR TRAVEL GUIDE

2024

PAT Z. WESTFIELD

Copyright ©2023 Pat Z. Westfield

All rights reserved.

Unauthorized reproduction, distribution or use of this content is strictly prohibited without the prior knowledge or written permission of the copyright owner.

TABLE OF CONTENTS

CHAPTER ONE 1

WELCOME TO ZANZIBAR 1
BRIEF HISTORY OF ZANZIBAR.. 1
CULTURAL DIVERSITY 4
Religion 5
GEOGRAPHY AND LOCATION 7
WEATHER AND CLIMATE 9
BEST TIME TO VISIT 10
ESSENTIAL THINGS TO PACK ON YOUR ZANZIBAR TRIP 13
VISA AND ENTRY REQUIREMENTS FOR ZANZIBAR 19
Visa Requirements 20
Entry Requirements 22

CHAPTER TWO 29

GETTING TO ZANZIBAR 29
AIR TRAVEL 29
GETTING AROUND ZANZIBAR 30
Public Transportation 30
Dala-Dalas 30
Tuk-Tuks 31
Taxi 33
Rental Cars 36
Motorcycles 39
Walking 42
Ferries 45
Domestic Flights 50

iii | Page

CHAPTER THREE..55

ACCOMMODATION OPTION IN ZANZIBAR......................55
Hotels and Resorts 55
Mid-Range Comfort..56
Guesthouses and Hostels 58
Airbnb and Vacation Rentals 60

CHAPTER FOUR...63

SIGHTSEEING AND ACTIVITIES..63
Exploring Stone Town 63
Forodhani Gardens 63
Cultural and Historical Sites 65
Palace Museum (Beit al-Sahel) 65
Anglican Cathedral of Christ 66
Darajani Market 66
Shangani Area..67
Maruhubi Palace Ruins 67
Livingstone House..68
Relaxing On the Beaches 69
Nungwi Beach..69
Kendwa Beach 72
Paje Beach 75
Jambiani Beach 76
Spice Plantations 78
Jozani Chwaka Bay National Park 81
Water Sports..84
Snorkeling and Diving..84
Sailing and Windsurfing 86
Kayaking and Paddleboarding 89
Big Game Fishing...91

Dolphin Watching 94
Kiteboarding 96
Jet Skiing and Parasailing 99

CHAPTER FIVE 103

CUISINE AND DINING 103
Traditional Zanzibari Dishes 103
Exploring Seafood Delights 105
International Cuisine 108
Street Food 110

CHAPTER SIX 115

SHOPPING IN ZANZIBAR 115
Markets 115
Darajani Market 115
Forodhani Night Market 118
Mkokotoni Fish Market 120
Souvenirs 123
Arts and Crafts 126
Maruhubi Arts & Crafts Centre 126
Zanzibar Curio Shop 128

CHAPTER SEVEN 131

NIGHTLIFE IN ZANZIBAR 131
Beach Parties 131
Live Music 133
Bars and Clubs 135

Unique Island Experiences 137

CHAPTER EIGHT 139

FESTIVALS AND EVENTS 139
Zanzibar International Film Festival (ZIFF) 139
Sauti za Busara Music Festival 142
Eid al-Fitr 145
Mwaka Kogwa Festival 147
Zanzibar Revolution Day 150
Zanzibar International Trade Fair (ZITF) 152

CHAPTER NINE 157

PRACTICAL INFORMATION 157
Currency Exchange 157
Time Zone 158
Weather 158
Electricity 158
Communication 159
Transportation 159
Wildlife and Conservation 160
Travel Insurance 160
Local Holidays and Festivals 160
Respect for the Environment 161
Banking and ATM 161
Festival and Event Calendar 161
Traveler's Health Kit 162
Tipping 162
Local Laws and Customs 163
Emergency Contacts 163

[vi]

Airport Departure Tax 165
Useful Websites and Resources for Your Zanzibar Trip.....166

CHAPTER TEN...171

MY MUST- DO LIST FOR AN UNFORGETTABLE
EXPERIENCE IN ZANZIBAR 171

CONCLUSION..181
PERSONAL NOTES..185

IMPORTANT NOTICE TO TRAVELERS

"THIS TRAVEL GUIDE DOES NOT CONTAIN IMAGES BECAUSE EVERY LOCATION IN HERE AS BEEN THOUGHTFULLY AND SCENICALLY DESCRIBED, MOREOVER

THE MOST BREATHTAKING IMAGES WILL BE THE ONES PAINTED BY YOUR VERY OWN EYES AS YOU VENTURE INTO A WORLD DIFFERENT FROM WHAT YOU ARE USED TO."

PAT Z. WESTFIELD

[x]

CHAPTER ONE

WELCOME TO ZANZIBAR

Welcome to Zanzibar, a captivating island paradise nestled in the heart of the Indian Ocean. This guide is your passport to an extraordinary journey through the enchanting world of Zanzibar. We'll delve into the island's rich history, its vibrant culture, and the breathtaking natural beauty that has made it a must-visit destination for travelers from around the globe.

Brief History of Zanzibar

Zanzibar's historical significance dates back to antiquity. Archaeological evidence suggests that the island has been inhabited for over a thousand years. Its strategic location along the East African coast made it a natural crossroads for trade.

Zanzibar's early history was shaped by traders from the Arabian Peninsula, Persia, and India who sailed the Indian Ocean seeking spices, ivory, and other precious goods. These interactions laid the foundation for the island's cultural diversity.

Arab Influence: Arab traders and merchants began to settle in Zanzibar around the 10th century. With them, they brought the Islamic faith, which remains a fundamental aspect of Zanzibar's identity today. The Swahili language, a fusion of Arabic and Bantu languages, also began to emerge during this period.

Cultural Fusion: The mingling of Arab, Indian, and African cultures in Zanzibar created a unique and vibrant culture. Swahili culture, with its distinctive art, music, and cuisine, reflects this fusion of influences.

Portuguese Colonial Era: In the 16th century, the Portuguese established control over Zanzibar, driven by the desire to monopolize the spice trade, particularly cloves. This period significantly shaped the island's economy and culture.

Over time, Portuguese influence waned as their control over the island weakened due to local resistance and other colonial powers vying for dominance in the region.

Omani Sultanate: In the late 17th century, Zanzibar fell under the rule of the Sultanate of Oman. This era marked a prosperous and transformative period for the island. The Omanis established the intricate labyrinthine architecture seen in Stone Town, which still stands today as a UNESCO World Heritage Site.

The Omanis recognized the potential of Zanzibar's fertile soil for spice cultivation. They initiated the widespread planting of cloves, cinnamon, nutmeg, and other spices that became the cornerstone of Zanzibar's economy.

The Abolition of the Slave Trade: Zanzibar's history is also marred by its involvement in the East African slave trade. The island served as a hub for the capture and sale of enslaved people, who endured immense suffering. The Zanzibar Slave Market, now a museum, serves as a somber reminder of this dark period.

Under British pressure and international condemnation, Sultan Barghash of Zanzibar formally abolished the slave trade in 1873. This marked a pivotal moment in the island's history and a step toward greater humanitarian awareness.

British Protectorate: In 1890, following the Heligoland-Zanzibar Treaty, Zanzibar became a British protectorate. The British colonial administration influenced the island's governance, infrastructure, and education system.

British colonial rule came to an end in 1963 when Zanzibar gained its independence.

Revolution and Independence: In January 1964, a revolution swept through Zanzibar, leading to the overthrow of the Sultan's government. This revolution had profound implications for the island's political landscape.

Union with Tanganyika: Later in 1964, Zanzibar and Tanganyika merged to form the United Republic of Tanzania. Zanzibar enjoys a degree of autonomy within this union.

Freddie Mercury's Legacy: Zanzibar proudly claims to be the birthplace of Freddie Mercury, one of rock music's most iconic figures. Mercury's childhood home in Stone Town is now a popular tourist attraction and a testament to the island's diverse cultural heritage.

In summary, Zanzibar's history is a captivating narrative of trade, cultural exchange, colonialism, and the struggle for independence. Exploring this history enriches your understanding of the island's present-day charm and its unique blend of cultures and traditions.

Cultural Diversity

Zanzibar's cultural landscape is a captivating mosaic of traditions and influences that have evolved over centuries. Its unique blend of Swahili, Arab, Persian, Indian, and European cultures is a testament to the island's historical significance as a crossroads of trade and civilization.

- **Swahili Influence:** At its core, Zanzibar embodies the Swahili culture, which has absorbed elements from various sources, resulting in a distinctive way of life. The Swahili people are known for their hospitality, strong sense of community, and deep-rooted traditions.

- **Arab and Persian Influences:** Arab and Persian traders left an indelible mark on Zanzibar, shaping its architecture, cuisine, and way of life. You'll find intricately designed buildings, fragrant spice markets, and a warm embrace of Islamic customs.

- **Indian and European Touches:** The Indian and European influences are also palpable in Zanzibar's culture. From aromatic Indian curries to remnants of British and Portuguese colonial legacies, these elements add depth to the island's identity.

Religion

Zanzibar is predominantly a Muslim island, and religion plays a central role in daily life.

Islam in Zanzibar: Islam is the dominant religion, with a majority of the population adhering to the Sunni branch. You'll encounter mosques throughout the island, each a center for spiritual and communal activities.

Islamic Customs: Visitors should be mindful of Islamic customs, such as modest clothing, particularly when visiting religious sites. It's also important to respect prayer times, which occur five times a day and are announced by the melodious call to prayer.

Festivals and Celebrations

Zanzibar hosts a variety of festivals and celebrations, providing a unique glimpse into local traditions and cultural expressions.

- **Zanzibar International Film Festival (ZIFF):** ZIFF is a prominent event that celebrates the arts, particularly African cinema. It's a platform for showcasing films from across the continent and beyond, attracting artists and film enthusiasts.
- **Mwaka Kogwa Festival:** This festival marks the Shirazi New Year and involves elaborate rituals, including mock fights symbolizing the defeat of one's enemies. It's a fascinating spectacle that offers insight into the island's historical roots.
- **Sauti za Busara:** This music festival brings together musicians from East Africa and beyond. It's a vibrant celebration of African rhythms and a great opportunity to experience the local music scene.

Traditional Clothing

Traditional clothing is an essential aspect of Zanzibar's cultural expression.

Kanzus and Kangas: Men often wear kanzus, long robes that provide comfort in the island's warm climate. Women adorn themselves with kangas, colorful sarongs that can convey messages or sentiments through their patterns and sayings.

Respecting Local Dress Codes: While visitors are not expected to wear traditional clothing, showing respect for local dress codes, especially when visiting religious sites, is appreciated. Dressing modestly, with shoulders and knees covered, is customary.

By embracing the cultural diversity and linguistic richness of Zanzibar, you'll not only navigate the island more effectively but also forge deeper connections with its friendly and welcoming inhabitants.

Geography and Location

Zanzibar is an idyllic tropical archipelago located in the Indian Ocean, off the eastern coast of Africa. It's a semi-autonomous region of Tanzania, consisting of the main island, Unguja, often referred to as Zanzibar Island, and numerous smaller islands and islets.

Zanzibar is strategically positioned at the crossroads of Africa, Asia, and the Middle East, which has greatly influenced its history, culture, and trade.

This equatorial location ensures a warm and tropical climate throughout the year, making it a favored destination for travelers seeking sun, sea, and sand.

Zanzibar is not just one island but a collection of islands and islets. The largest and most populous is Unguja, followed by Pemba Island to the north. There are also numerous smaller islands and sandbanks scattered around the archipelago, each offering its unique charm and natural beauty.

Coastline: Zanzibar boasts an extensive coastline that stretches for over 1,600 kilometers (about 1,000 miles). This coastline is adorned with some of the world's most beautiful beaches, fringed with powdery white sand and framed by the crystal-clear waters of the Indian Ocean.

Landscape: The landscape of Zanzibar is diverse, featuring everything from lush tropical forests to rolling hills and fertile farmlands. Inland, you'll find picturesque villages and plantations growing spices like cloves, nutmeg, and cinnamon.

Coral Reefs: The surrounding waters of Zanzibar are famous for their vibrant coral reefs, which are a haven for marine life. Snorkeling and diving enthusiasts flock here to explore these underwater ecosystems, teeming with colorful fish and other marine creatures.

Historical Stone Town: The capital of Zanzibar, Stone Town, is a UNESCO World Heritage Site known for its narrow streets, historic buildings, and a unique blend of Arabian, Indian, and African architecture.

Zanzibar is easily accessible by air and sea. The Abeid Amani Karume International Airport on Unguja Island serves as the primary gateway for international travelers. Additionally, several ferries operate between the mainland city of Dar es Salaam and Zanzibar, making it accessible by sea as well.

In summary, Zanzibar's geographical location, diverse landscape, and strategic position in the Indian Ocean make it a captivating destination for travelers seeking a mix of culture, history, and natural beauty.

Weather And Climate

Zanzibar's weather and climate play a pivotal role in shaping the island's charm and allure. Understanding the weather patterns will help you plan your trip effectively.

Zanzibar's climate is one of its most enticing features, attracting travelers year-round with its tropical allure. The island's climate is characterized by warm temperatures and distinct wet and dry seasons, each offering a unique experience for visitors.

- **Dry Season (June to October):** Zanzibar's dry season is the prime time to bask in the island's beauty. From June to October, the weather is exceptionally inviting. Days are characterized by clear, azure skies and abundant sunshine. Humidity levels drop, creating a comfortable atmosphere for exploration. Daytime temperatures typically range from a pleasant 77°F (25°C) to a balmy 90°F (32°C), making it perfect for outdoor activities like snorkeling, diving, and sightseeing.

- **Wet Season (November to May):** The wet season, which spans from November to May, brings a different kind of charm to Zanzibar. While this period sees occasional heavy rain showers, they are usually short-lived, allowing the island to maintain its lush, green landscapes. The rain is a vital lifeline for the island's rich flora, making it a paradise for nature enthusiasts. The wet season also sees slightly warmer temperatures, with daytime highs ranging from 82°F (28°C) to 91°F (33°C). Although it may be humid, the landscape's vibrancy during this time is a sight to behold.

Rainfall:

- **Wet Season Rainfall:** The wet season is when Zanzibar experiences its heaviest rainfall, particularly from March to May. While the rains can be intense, they often occur in the form of short, refreshing showers, interspersed with periods of sunshine. It's worth noting that Zanzibar's north and east coasts typically receive more rain than the drier west coast.

Best Time to Visit

Choosing the right time to visit Zanzibar can greatly enhance your overall experience on this captivating island. Zanzibar's weather, events, and even the number of tourists can vary significantly from season to season. Here's a comprehensive guide to help you decide the best time to plan your trip.

June to October (Dry Season)

- **Weather:** This period is often regarded as the best time to visit Zanzibar. The weather is characterized by warm, sunny days with clear skies and lower humidity levels. Rainfall is minimal, and the temperatures are comfortable, ranging from 77°F (25°C) to 90°F (32°C).
- **Activities:** The dry season is perfect for outdoor activities such as swimming, snorkeling, diving, and exploring the island's historical sites. You can also enjoy the vibrant nightlife without worrying about rain.
- **Wildlife:** This is an excellent time for wildlife enthusiasts, as marine life is thriving, and the visibility for diving and snorkeling is at its best.
- **Crowds:** Expect larger crowds during this high tourist season, especially in popular areas like Stone Town and the northern beaches.

November to May (Wet Season)

- **Weather:** The wet season in Zanzibar is characterized by brief but intense rain showers, typically in the afternoon or evening. While it's the rainy season, it's worth noting that Zanzibar remains lush and green during this time. Daytime temperatures range from 82°F (28°C) to 91°F (33°C), and humidity levels are higher.

- **Activities:** While the rain may interrupt outdoor activities briefly, there are still plenty of things to do. The landscape is beautifully green, making it an ideal time for nature walks, spice plantation tours, and exploring cultural attractions. Plus, accommodations tend to be more affordable, and you'll encounter fewer tourists.
- **Wildlife:** Birdwatchers will appreciate the wet season as it's a fantastic time to spot migratory birds.
- **Crowds:** The wet season is the quieter time of the year, with fewer tourists, which can be perfect if you prefer a more tranquil experience.

Festivals and Events

Consider timing your visit to coincide with one of Zanzibar's vibrant festivals:

- **Sauti za Busara (February):** This world-renowned music festival celebrates African music and culture and is a must-attend event for music lovers.
- **Zanzibar International Film Festival (July):** If you have an interest in cinema, this festival showcases African and international films, along with cultural exhibitions and workshops.

- **Eid al-Fitr (varies, based on the Islamic lunar calendar):** Experience the joyous celebrations and feasts of Eid in Zanzibar, a predominantly Muslim island.

Overall, he best time to visit Zanzibar ultimately depends on your interests and preferences. If you're a sunseeker who wants to make the most of the beaches and water sports, the dry season from June to October is ideal. However, if you prefer a quieter and more budget-friendly experience with lush landscapes, consider the wet season from November to May.

Whichever time you choose, Zanzibar's unique charm and cultural richness will ensure you have a memorable and enchanting experience on this Indian Ocean gem.

Essential Things to Pack On Your Zanzibar Trip

To make the most of your trip and ensure your comfort, it's crucial to pack wisely. This guide will walk you through the essential items to include in your suitcase, helping you navigate the unique blend of adventure and relaxation that Zanzibar offers. From sun protection to clothing essentials, we've got you covered for an amazing island experience.

Travel Documents

- **Passport**: Make sure your passport is valid for at least six months beyond your planned return date. Check your expiration date well in advance of your trip.

- **Visa and Entry Documents**: Research the visa requirements for Zanzibar based on your nationality and the purpose of your visit. Ensure you have all necessary visas and permits before departure.

- **Travel Insurance**: Purchase comprehensive travel insurance that covers medical emergencies, trip cancellations, and lost belongings. Carry physical copies of your policy and have the contact information for emergency assistance readily accessible.

- **Flight Tickets**: Keep both digital and physical copies of your flight tickets, including any electronic boarding passes.

Money and Banking

- **Local Currency**: While major currencies like USD and EUR are accepted in Zanzibar, it's a good idea to carry some Tanzanian Shillings for smaller purchases and places that might not accept foreign currency.

- **Credit/Debit Cards**: Notify your bank of your travel dates to avoid card issues due to international transactions. Carry at least two cards from different networks as a backup.

- **ATM Card**: Zanzibar has ATMs, so you can withdraw local currency as needed. Inform your bank about your travel plans to prevent your card from being blocked.

Health and Safety

- **Prescription Medications**: Ensure you have an ample supply of any prescription medications you take regularly. Carry them in their original containers and bring a copy of your prescription.

- **First Aid Kit**: Include essentials like adhesive bandages, pain relievers, antiseptic wipes, anti-diarrheal medication, and any specific medications you might need.

- **Insect Repellent**: Zanzibar has a tropical climate, and mosquitos can be a concern. Pack a good quality insect repellent with DEET.

- **Sunscreen**: The sun in Zanzibar can be intense. Bring a broad-spectrum sunscreen with a high SPF rating to protect your skin from UV radiation.

- **Travel Insurance Information**: Have your travel insurance details handy, including policy numbers and emergency contact numbers. It's crucial for quick assistance in case of accidents or illnesses.

Electronics

- **Phone and Charger**: A mobile phone with a charger is essential for communication and emergencies. Consider getting a local SIM card for data and calls.

- **Adapter/Converter**: Zanzibar uses Type D and Type G sockets, so bring the appropriate adapter to charge your electronics.

- **Camera and Accessories**: If you're a photography enthusiast, don't forget your camera, extra batteries, memory cards, and a protective case.

- **Headphones**: Whether for listening to music, podcasts, or in-flight entertainment, headphones will keep you entertained during your journey.

Clothing

- **Lightweight Clothing**: Pack breathable fabrics like cotton and linen to stay comfortable in Zanzibar's warm and humid climate.

- **Swimwear**: Essential for enjoying the stunning beaches and crystal-clear waters.

- **Comfortable Walking Shoes**: Zanzibar offers plenty of opportunities for exploring. Bring comfortable walking or hiking shoes, depending on your planned activities.

- **Rain Jacket**: Consider a lightweight, packable rain jacket for unexpected tropical rain showers.

- **Hat and Sunglasses**: Protect yourself from the strong sun with a wide-brimmed hat and quality sunglasses with UV protection.

- **Sarong or Cover-up**: Useful for covering up when visiting conservative areas or as a beach cover-up.

- **Long-sleeved Clothing**: Lightweight, long-sleeved clothing can provide protection from the sun and insects, especially during cooler evenings.

Toiletries

- Toothbrush and Toothpaste

- Shampoo and Conditioner
- Soap or Body Wash
- Razor
- Deodorant

Miscellaneous

- **Travel Pillow**: A neck pillow can make long journeys more comfortable and help you get some rest on flights or road trips.
- **Reusable Water Bottle**: Stay hydrated by refilling your bottle with clean, safe water and reduce plastic waste.
- **Travel Backpack or Daypack**: Handy for day trips, carrying essentials, and keeping your hands free while exploring.
- **Travel Guides and Maps**: Plan your adventures and navigate unfamiliar places with the help of travel books, maps, or digital guides.
- **Snacks**: Pack non-perishable snacks like granola bars, nuts, or dried fruit for energy during long journeys or when local food options are limited.
- **Travel Locks**: Secure your luggage and valuables with combination or key locks.

- **Travel Umbrella**: Be prepared for sudden rain showers, especially if you visit during the rainy season.

- **Laundry Bag**: Keep your dirty clothes separate from clean ones to maintain organization.

- **Ziplock Bags**: Useful for organizing toiletries, protecting electronics from moisture, and storing snacks.

- **Local SIM Card**: Consider getting a local SIM card for data, local calls, and navigation.

Entertainment

- **Books or E-reader**: Bring reading material for leisurely reading during downtime.

- **Travel Journal**: Document your experiences, jot down notes, and keep a record of your journey.

Remember that while it's important to be well-prepared, it's also essential to pack light and efficiently. Consider the specific activities you plan to do in Zanzibar and the duration of your stay to tailor your packing list accordingly.

Visa and Entry Requirements for Zanzibar

Before embarking on your journey to the exotic island of Zanzibar, it's crucial to understand the visa and entry regulations to ensure a smooth and hassle-free experience. Zanzibar, as part of Tanzania, has its own set of requirements for visitors based on nationality, the purpose of travel, and the length of stay. This section provides a comprehensive guide to help you navigate the necessary documentation and processes.

Visa Requirements

Most travelers to Zanzibar need a tourist visa to enter. Here are key points to consider:

Tourist Visa

Most travelers to Zanzibar need a tourist visa to enter. Here are key points to consider:

- **Visa Types**: Zanzibar offers both single-entry and multiple-entry tourist visas.
- **Duration**: Single-entry visas typically allow stays of up to 90 days, while multiple-entry visas are valid for a longer period.
- **Application**: You can apply for a tourist visa at Zanzibar's embassies or consulates in your home

country or obtain one on arrival at Zanzibar's airports or border crossings.

- **Visa Fees**: Visa fees vary depending on your nationality and the type of visa. It's advisable to check the current fees before your trip.

Visa on Arrival

Zanzibar provides a visa-on-arrival option for citizens of many countries. However, it's essential to verify your eligibility and requirements in advance.

Visa Extension

If you wish to extend your stay in Zanzibar, you can apply for a visa extension at the immigration office on the island. Extensions are typically granted for 30 days, and you must apply before your initial visa expires.

Visa Exemptions:

While most travelers to Zanzibar are required to obtain a visa, there are specific exemptions based on your nationality and the purpose of your visit. These exemptions are subject to change, so it's crucial to verify the current status before planning your trip. Here are some common categories of visa exemptions:

East African Community (EAC) Citizens: Citizens of EAC member states, including Kenya, Uganda, Rwanda, Burundi, and South Sudan, can enter Zanzibar without a visa for short visits.

They are generally allowed to stay for up to 90 days.

Commonwealth Countries: Some Commonwealth countries enjoy visa exemptions for visits to Zanzibar.

Travelers from countries like the United Kingdom, Canada, Australia, and India often do not require a visa for tourist stays of up to 90 days.

Special Agreements

Zanzibar may have bilateral agreements with certain countries that grant visa exemptions.

These agreements often apply to specific categories of travelers, such as students or business professionals.

It's important to note that the specific conditions and duration of visa exemptions can vary. Even if you qualify for an exemption.

Passport Requirements

Ensure your passport meets the following criteria:

- **Validity**: Your passport should be valid for at least six months beyond your intended departure date from Zanzibar.

- **Blank Pages**: It should have blank pages for visa stamps.

Entry Requirements

When traveling to Zanzibar, it's essential to meet certain entry requirements to ensure a seamless and hassle-free arrival. Here are the key entry requirements to keep in mind:

Return/Onward Ticket

To enter Zanzibar, you will typically be required to show proof of a return or onward ticket. This ticket should demonstrate that you have plans to leave Zanzibar within the permitted duration of your visa or visa exemption.

- **Why It's Important:** Immigration officials use this requirement to ensure that you do not intend to overstay your allowed period in Zanzibar. Having a printed or electronic copy of your flight itinerary readily accessible is advisable.

Proof of Accommodation

You may also be asked to provide evidence of your accommodation arrangements while in Zanzibar. This can be in the form of a hotel reservation confirmation or a letter of invitation from a host, if you're staying with a local resident.

- **Why It's Important:** Immigration authorities want to verify that you have a place to stay during your visit and that you're not entering the country with uncertain housing arrangements.

Other Supporting Documents

- **Travel Insurance:** While not always a strict requirement, having travel insurance is highly recommended. It can cover unexpected medical expenses, trip cancellations, and other emergencies during your stay in Zanzibar.

- **Proof of Funds:** Immigration officials may inquire about your financial means to support yourself during your stay. This could include bank statements or proof of sufficient cash or credit.

Yellow Fever Vaccination

Depending on your country of origin and your travel history, you may need to provide a valid Yellow Fever vaccination certificate. This requirement is primarily aimed at travelers arriving from or who have recently visited countries with a risk of Yellow Fever transmission.

- **Why It's Important:** Zanzibar takes this precaution to prevent the introduction and spread of Yellow Fever, a potentially serious disease.

Customs Declaration

Upon arrival, you may be asked to complete a customs declaration form. This form typically asks about items you're bringing into the country, including currency, goods for sale, and items of cultural significance.

- **Why It's Important:** Accurate completion of this form is crucial, as it helps customs officials determine whether you need to pay duties or taxes on certain items.

Immigration and Health Forms:

You may be required to fill out immigration and health declaration forms. These forms collect basic information about your identity, travel history, and any potential health risks.

- **Why It's Important:** These forms help authorities manage immigration and health-related matters, including tracking the spread of infectious diseases.

Compliance with Local Laws and Regulations:

While not a document, it's vital to be aware of and adhere to local laws and regulations. Respect cultural norms, obey local customs, and follow any specific rules in place in Zanzibar.

- **Why It's Important:** Complying with local laws and respecting the culture of your host country is not only legally required but also a sign of respect for the local community.

By being prepared and ensuring you meet these entry requirements, you'll have a smoother and more enjoyable experience upon your arrival in Zanzibar. Additionally, it's always wise to check for any specific entry requirements that may apply to your nationality or the purpose of your visit before traveling.

Health and Travel Insurance

While not mandatory, it's highly recommended to have comprehensive health and travel insurance that covers medical expenses and emergency evacuation during your stay in Zanzibar.

Customs Regulations

Familiarize yourself with Zanzibar's customs regulations, including duty-free allowances for personal items and restrictions on specific goods like drugs and wildlife products.

Departure Tax

Upon leaving Zanzibar, you may be required to pay a departure tax, typically included in your airfare. Verify this with your airline when booking your tickets.

Important Tips

- **Documentation**: Always carry copies of your passport, visa, and other essential documents while exploring Zanzibar.

- **Visa Changes**: Visa regulations can change, so stay updated with the latest information from official sources or your nearest Zanzibari embassy or consulate.

- **Check with Airlines**: Confirm visa and entry requirements with your airline before departure, as some airlines may have specific guidelines.

By understanding and adhering to these visa and entry requirements, you'll be well-prepared to embark on your Zanzibar adventure with confidence. Remember that visa and entry conditions can change, so it's advisable to verify the latest information before your trip.

CHAPTER TWO

GETTING TO ZANZIBAR

Zanzibar, with its pristine beaches and rich culture, is a traveler's dream. To ensure your journey is smooth and enjoyable, let's delve into the details of getting to this exotic paradise and navigating the island once you're there.

Air Travel

Zanzibar International Airport (ZNZ) is your primary entry point to the island. It operates as a well-connected hub for international flights, making it convenient for travelers from various parts of the world to access this exotic destination. Airlines like Emirates, Ethiopian Airlines, and Qatar Airways offer flights to Zanzibar.

Connecting Flights: If you cannot find a direct flight to Zanzibar from your location, consider connecting through major African cities like Nairobi, Dar es Salaam, or Addis Ababa. These cities often have multiple flights to Zanzibar, allowing you to plan your journey with flexibility.

Getting Around Zanzibar

Getting around Zanzibar is an adventure in itself. The island offers various transportation options:

Public Transportation

Public transportation in Zanzibar offers an authentic and budget-friendly way to explore the island's towns, villages, and natural wonders. Here's what you need to know about using public transport during your visit:

Dala-Dalas

Dala-dalas are small, colorful minibusses that serve as the primary mode of public transportation in Zanzibar. These minibusses are an integral part of daily life for locals and are often adorned with vibrant artwork and slogans.

Routes and Stops: Dala-dalas operate on various routes across the island, connecting towns, villages, and popular tourist destinations. While they may not have official bus stops, you can usually catch one at a designated area or by flagging it down along the route.

Fares and Payment: Fares are relatively low, making dala-dalas an economical choice for travelers. Pay the fare directly to the conductor when you board. Keep in mind that exact change is often appreciated.

Crowded but Charming: Dala-dalas can get crowded, providing an excellent opportunity to interact with locals and experience Zanzibar's culture firsthand. Be prepared for close quarters, especially during peak hours.

Timings: Dala-dalas typically operate from early morning until late evening. However, schedules can be flexible, so it's a good idea to inquire about departure times if you have specific plans.

Tuk-Tuks

When you step onto the colorful streets of Zanzibar's towns and cities, one mode of transportation stands out - the iconic tuk-tuk. These three-wheeled vehicles, also known as "auto-rickshaws" or "tricycles," play a significant role in local transportation and offer tourists a unique and enjoyable way to explore the island.

Tuk-tuks are a convenient and affordable way to get around Zanzibar, especially within towns and cities. Here's how to use them effectively:

Hailing a Tuk-Tuk: You can easily spot tuk-tuks parked along streets or at busy intersections. To hail one, simply raise your hand, and if it's available, the driver will pull over.

Negotiating Fares: Unlike taxis, tuk-tuks in Zanzibar typically do not have meters. It's essential to negotiate the fare with the driver before starting your journey. Prices can vary, so be sure to agree on the cost upfront.

Short Journeys: Tuk-tuks are ideal for short trips within towns or cities, such as getting from your accommodation to a nearby restaurant or tourist attraction.

Enjoy the Ride: Riding in a tuk-tuk is an experience in itself. You'll have a front-row seat to observe local life, architecture, and the vibrant atmosphere of Zanzibar's streets.

Payment: Be prepared to pay in cash (Tanzanian Shilling is preferred), as tuk-tuks rarely accept credit cards.

Safety and Tips for Riding Tuk-Tuks

- Always agree on the fare before setting off on your journey.
- Hold on to your belongings and keep them secure, as tuk-tuks are open on the sides.
- Be cautious when disembarking, as tuk-tuks are low to the ground, and the step down can be steep.

Overall, embrace the open-air experience, enjoy the local sights and sounds, and let the friendly tuk-tuk drivers take you on a memorable journey through this exotic island paradise.

Taxi

Taxis are a convenient and widely-used mode of transportation in Zanzibar, offering flexibility and ease of access for travelers exploring the island. Here's everything you need to know about taxis in Zanzibar:

Types of Taxis

In Zanzibar, you'll encounter two primary types of taxis:

1. Airport Taxis: These taxis are typically stationed at Zanzibar International Airport (ZNZ) and are readily available for arriving passengers. They provide a convenient way to reach your accommodation from the airport.

2. Town Taxis: Within towns and cities on the island, you'll find town taxis. These are often smaller vehicles, such as Toyota Taxis or Suzuki Taxis, and can be hailed from the streets or found at taxi stands.

Hiring a Taxi

Hailing a taxi in Zanzibar is a straightforward process:

At the Airport: Upon arrival at Zanzibar International Airport, you'll find a designated taxi rank. Airport taxis are usually operated by a cooperative or association, ensuring fair pricing.

In Towns and Cities: In urban areas like Stone Town, you can flag down a taxi from the roadside. Look for vehicles with taxi signs or ask your accommodation to arrange one for you.

Negotiating Fares

It's important to note that taxis in Zanzibar might not always use meters, so fares are typically negotiated in advance. Here are some tips for fare negotiation:

Ask Locals: Before negotiating a fare, it can be helpful to ask locals or your accommodation staff for an idea of what the fare should be for your intended journey.

Negotiate Clearly: When you approach a taxi, be sure to negotiate the fare clearly before getting in. It's common to haggle a bit, so don't hesitate to counteroffer if the initial price seems high.

Agree on Currency: Specify the currency you'll be using for payment to avoid confusion. While the Tanzanian Shilling (TZS) is the local currency, some drivers may accept US dollars or Euros.

Keep Small Change: It's advisable to carry small denominations of local currency to make paying the fare more convenient.

Shared Taxis

In Zanzibar, shared taxis, where multiple passengers travel together to the same or nearby destinations, are common. This practice helps reduce costs and is often used for short journeys within towns and cities.

Taxi Safety

While taxis in Zanzibar are generally safe, it's essential to take some precautions:

- **Confirm the Fare:** Always confirm the fare before starting your journey to avoid disputes at the end of the ride.
- **Driver Identification:** Take note of the driver's identification or license displayed in the vehicle, especially if you have any concerns.
- **Share Your Location:** When using a taxi, share your location and expected arrival time with someone you trust, especially if you're traveling alone.

Tips for a Smooth Taxi Ride

- **Be Patient:** Traffic in Zanzibar can be congested, especially in urban areas. Allow extra time for your journey, especially if you have a scheduled activity.
- **Carry Cash:** Taxis in Zanzibar typically accept cash payments, so ensure you have sufficient local currency on hand.
- **Local Knowledge:** Some taxi drivers may offer valuable insights into local attractions or suggest lesser-known places to visit. Don't hesitate to ask for recommendations.

- **Bargain Politely:** While it's common to negotiate fares, remember to be polite and respectful during the bargaining process.

Taxis in Zanzibar are a convenient and flexible way to explore the island. By understanding the types of taxis available, how to hire one, and what to expect in terms of fare negotiation, you can ensure a smooth and enjoyable transportation experience during your visit to this tropical paradise.

Rental Cars

Renting a car in Zanzibar can be a fantastic way to explore this beautiful island at your own pace. Here's everything you need to know about renting cars in Zanzibar:

Why Rent a Car in Zanzibar?

1. **Independence:** Renting a car provides you with the freedom to explore Zanzibar's stunning landscapes, beaches, and attractions at your own leisurely pace. You won't be tied to public transportation schedules or dependent on taxi availability.

2. **Off-the-Beaten-Path Adventures:** Zanzibar boasts not only popular tourist spots but also hidden gems in its interior. A rental car allows you

to reach remote villages, spice farms, and natural reserves that may be less accessible by other means.

3. **Convenience:** Car rentals offer convenience, especially if you're traveling with a group or have a lot of luggage. You can easily transport your belongings and travel comfortably.

Renting a Car: Key Information

1. **Driving License:** To rent a car in Zanzibar, you generally need a valid international driver's license and, in some cases, a national driving license from your home country. Always check the specific requirements with the rental agency.

2. **Minimum Age:** Rental car companies typically require drivers to be at least 21 years old, and some may have a higher age requirement. Drivers under 25 may incur additional fees.

3. **Insurance:** Verify the insurance coverage provided by the rental agency. Basic insurance is usually included, but you may want to consider additional coverage for extra peace of mind.

4. **Road Conditions:** While major roads are generally well-maintained, some rural and off-road areas may have rougher conditions. If you plan to explore these areas, consider renting a 4x4 or a car with higher ground clearance.

Rental Car Agencies in Zanzibar

There are several rental car agencies on the island, and it's essential to choose a reputable one. Here are some popular options:

- **Major International Agencies:** Companies like Avis, Hertz, and Europcar have a presence in Zanzibar and offer reliable service with a range of vehicle options.

- **Local Agencies:** You can also consider local rental agencies, which may offer competitive rates and personalized service. However, do your research and read reviews to ensure their reliability.

Tips for Renting a Car in Zanzibar

1. **Book in Advance:** Especially during the peak tourist season, it's wise to book your rental car in advance to secure the vehicle of your choice.

2. **Inspect the Car:** Before accepting the car, thoroughly inspect it for any existing damage. Note and document any scratches, dents, or issues with the rental agency to avoid disputes upon return.

3. **Driving Habits:** Drive cautiously in Zanzibar, as road conditions and local traffic norms may differ

from what you're accustomed to. Speed limits are generally lower, and roads can be narrow.

4. **Navigation Apps:** GPS navigation apps like Google Maps can be a valuable tool for finding your way around the island. However, be aware that they may not always have updated maps for remote areas.

5. **Parking:** In cities like Stone Town, parking can be a challenge. Look for designated parking areas and be prepared to pay a small fee.

6. **Local Traffic Rules:** Familiarize yourself with local traffic rules, including the requirement to drive on the left side of the road.

Cost of Renting a Car

Rental car prices in Zanzibar vary depending on the type of vehicle, duration of rental, and the rental agency. Expect to pay between $30 to $100 or more per day for a standard car, with discounts available for longer rental periods.

Overall, renting a car in Zanzibar can enhance your travel experience by allowing you to explore the island independently. Whether you're cruising along the scenic coastline or venturing into the lush interior, a rental car offers the freedom to make the most of your Zanzibar adventure.

Motorcycles

Motorcycle travel offers a unique and exhilarating experience, allowing you to discover Zanzibar at your own pace. Here's a comprehensive guide to motorcycle travel on this beautiful island:

Renting Motorcycles

Zanzibar boasts several reputable motorcycle rental agencies that cater to adventurous travelers. When renting, it's crucial to choose a company with a good track record for maintenance and safety. Some agencies also offer guided motorcycle tours, providing a hassle-free way to explore the island.

Requirements: Generally, you will need a valid international driver's license to rent a motorcycle in Zanzibar. Some agencies may require you to have prior motorcycle riding experience and be at least 18 or 21 years old.

Safety Gear: Ensure that you are provided with appropriate safety gear, including helmets, when renting a motorcycle. Your safety should be a top priority.

Riding in Zanzibar

1. Road Conditions: Zanzibar's road conditions can vary significantly. While major roads are generally in good shape, some rural and less-traveled routes may be bumpy or unpaved. Exercise caution and adapt your speed to the road conditions.

2. Local Traffic: Traffic in Zanzibar, especially in urban areas, can be chaotic and follow its own rhythm. Expect pedestrians, bicycles, tuk-tuks, and other vehicles to share the road. Defensive driving is essential.

3. Wildlife Caution: Zanzibar is home to a variety of wildlife, including monkeys and livestock. Keep an eye out for animals that might unexpectedly cross the road, particularly in rural areas.

4. Fuel: Gasoline stations are generally available across the island, especially in larger towns. Ensure you know the location of nearby stations before embarking on long rides, as remote areas may have limited fuel options.

5. Navigation: GPS navigation apps like Google Maps can be helpful for navigating the island. However, note that in more rural areas, cell phone reception may be limited.

Safety and Considerations

1. Riding Experience: If you're new to motorcycle riding, it's advisable to take a lesson or practice in a safe area before venturing onto Zanzibar's roads.

2. Protective Gear: Always wear appropriate protective gear, including a helmet, gloves, long pants, and closed-toe shoes. The tropical sun can be intense, so consider sun protection as well.

3. Insurance: Check whether your motorcycle rental includes insurance coverage, and understand the terms and conditions, including liability coverage and deductibles.

4. Local Regulations: Familiarize yourself with Zanzibar's traffic rules and regulations, including speed limits, and respect local laws and customs.

With the wind in your hair and the freedom to explore, it's an adventure you won't soon forget. Just remember to prioritize safety, adhere to local regulations, and savor the remarkable sights and sounds of this enchanting destination from the saddle of your motorcycle.

Walking

One of the simplest yet most immersive ways to experience Zanzibar is by walking. If you're strolling through the narrow, winding streets of Stone Town or exploring the serene countryside, walking allows you to connect with the culture, people, and stunning natural landscapes of this island paradise. Here's your comprehensive guide to walking in Zanzibar:

Exploring Stone Town on Foot

Stone Town, a UNESCO World Heritage Site, is best discovered on foot. This historic town is a labyrinth of narrow streets, ancient buildings, and hidden courtyards. As you walk, you'll encounter architectural marvels, including intricately carved wooden doors, elegant balconies, and mosques with towering minarets.

Forodhani Gardens: A pleasant walk along the seafront promenade will lead you to Forodhani Gardens. In the evening, this area comes alive with street food vendors offering local delicacies. Try Zanzibar pizza or freshly grilled seafood while enjoying the sea breeze.

Spice Tours: Consider booking a guided spice tour where you can walk through spice plantations. Guides will teach you about the various spices grown on the island, such as cloves, vanilla, and cinnamon. This aromatic journey engages all your senses.

Coastal Walks

Beaches: Zanzibar boasts some of the world's most beautiful beaches. Take leisurely walks along the soft, white sands of Nungwi Beach in the north or the more tranquil Kendwa Beach. Early morning or late afternoon walks offer breathtaking sunrises and sunsets.

Jambiani and Paje: On the southeast coast, Jambiani and Paje offer pristine stretches of beach for long, peaceful walks. Explore tidal pools, watch local fishermen at work, and admire the traditional dhow boats lining the shore.

Mangrove Walks: In areas like Chwaka Bay and Jozani Forest, guided mangrove walks are an eco-friendly way to experience Zanzibar's unique coastal ecosystems. Walk along elevated boardwalks and observe the diverse marine life, including crabs and bird species.

Exploring Rural Zanzibar

Villages: To gain insight into the island's local culture, consider taking a guided walk through rural villages. You'll have the opportunity to meet friendly locals, witness traditional crafts, and perhaps even join in on daily activities like farming or cooking.

Spice Farms: Beyond the beaches, Zanzibar's interior is filled with lush landscapes and spice plantations. Explore these areas on foot, guided by locals who will share their knowledge of spice cultivation and offer you fresh fruit from the trees.

Safety and Considerations

Dress Code: While Zanzibar is relatively relaxed in terms of dress code, it's respectful to cover your shoulders and knees when walking through villages or visiting religious sites. In more touristy areas, beachwear is acceptable.

Sun Protection: Zanzibar's sun can be intense. Wear sunscreen, a hat, and sunglasses, and carry a reusable water bottle to stay hydrated during your walks.

Wildlife: In rural areas, you might encounter wildlife such as monkeys or birds. Enjoy observing them from a distance, but never feed or approach them, as this can disrupt their natural behavior.

Local Interaction: Zanzibaris are generally friendly and welcoming. Engage in polite conversation and ask for permission before taking photos of people, especially in rural communities.

Whether you're meandering through the historic streets of Stone Town or taking peaceful beach walks, exploring on foot provides an authentic and unforgettable experience of this tropical paradise.

Ferries

There are basically two kinds of ferries:

1. Passenger Ferries:

- **Overview:** Passenger ferries are the backbone of inter-island and mainland transportation in Zanzibar. They are designed to carry passengers comfortably across the crystal-clear waters of the Indian Ocean.

- **Destinations:** Passenger ferries connect Zanzibar to several destinations, including Dar es Salaam, Pemba Island, and Mafia Island, making them vital for both local commuters and tourists.

- **Operators:** Notable operators include Azam Marine, Coastal Aviation, and Sea Link. These operators maintain a fleet of well-maintained ferries, ensuring safe and reliable journeys.

- **Frequency:** Passenger ferries often run several times a day, providing flexibility in travel plans.

- **Duration:** The duration of the ferry ride varies depending on the destination. For example, the journey between Zanzibar and Dar es Salaam typically takes between 1.5 to 2.5 hours. The comfort level may vary depending on the class of ticket, with some ferries offering economy and VIP sections.

Cargo Ferries:

Overview: Cargo ferries are primarily responsible for transporting goods and commodities between the islands of Zanzibar and the Tanzanian mainland. These ferries may also allow passengers, though the conditions might be less comfortable compared to passenger ferries.

Travelers can often board cargo ferries alongside the cargo, providing an opportunity for a more authentic, albeit basic, experience of local maritime life.

1. **Zanzibar to Dar es Salaam:**

   - **Overview:** The ferry route between Zanzibar and Dar es Salaam on the Tanzanian mainland is one of the busiest and most popular routes.

   - **Operators:** Several ferry companies operate on this route, including Azam Marine, Sea Link, and Fast Ferries, offering travelers multiple options to choose from.

   - **Duration:** The journey duration typically ranges from 1.5 to 2.5 hours, making it a convenient choice for travelers moving between Zanzibar and the mainland.

2. **Zanzibar to Pemba Island:**

   - **Overview:** Pemba Island, the less-visited counterpart to Zanzibar, is accessible via passenger ferries. The journey offers passengers views of the Indian Ocean and glimpses of coastal life.

   - **Duration:** The ferry ride between Zanzibar and Pemba Island takes approximately 4 to 5 hours, providing ample time to relax and enjoy the scenic voyage.

3. Zanzibar to Mafia Island:

- **Overview:** Ferries also connect Zanzibar with the stunning Mafia Island, known for its marine biodiversity and opportunities for diving and snorkeling.
- **Duration:** The journey from Zanzibar to Mafia Island takes approximately 5 to 6 hours, allowing travelers to appreciate the beauty of the Indian Ocean.

Tips for Ferry Travel

1. **Booking in Advance:** Especially during peak tourist seasons, it's advisable to book ferry tickets in advance. Many ferry companies offer online booking services or have ticket offices at the terminals.
2. **Arrive Early:** Arriving at the ferry terminal well in advance of departure is recommended. Boarding procedures, including ticket verification and security checks, can take time, and ferry companies typically start boarding early to ensure timely departures.
3. **Seasickness:** If you're susceptible to seasickness, consider taking appropriate precautions. Over-the-counter motion sickness medication can be helpful. Choose a seat near the center of the ferry for more stability.

4. **Luggage:** Keep a close eye on your luggage during the journey. While ferries are generally safe, it's wise to take precautions to safeguard your belongings.

5. **Weather:** The schedules of ferries can be affected by adverse weather conditions, particularly during the rainy season. Be prepared for potential delays, and keep abreast of any announcements or updates from the ferry company.

6. **Respect Local Customs:** While ferries are a common mode of transportation for tourists, it's essential to respect local customs and adhere to guidelines provided by the ferry operators. This includes dressing modestly and following any specific instructions.

Safety Considerations

Traveling by ferry in Zanzibar is generally safe, but it's essential to familiarize yourself with safety procedures:

- **Life Jackets:** On board, find out where life jackets are located and how to use them. They are essential safety equipment and should be worn in the event of an emergency.

- **Emergency Exits:** Be aware of the locations of emergency exits and familiarize yourself with the procedures for using them, especially if you are traveling with children.

- **Follow Instructions:** Pay close attention to safety instructions provided by the ferry crew, and follow them diligently in case of an emergency. Ferry crews are well-trained to respond to various situations, and it's crucial to cooperate with them.

Zanzibar's ferries not only provide a means of transportation but also offer a unique perspective of the stunning Indian Ocean.

Domestic Flights

Domestic flights within Zanzibar offer travelers a convenient and efficient way to explore this diverse island. Whether you're seeking a quick transfer to a remote beach, a visit to one of Zanzibar's neighboring islands, or an alternative to long road journeys, domestic flights have you covered.

Domestic Airports in Zanzibar

1. **Zanzibar International Airport (ZNZ):** Although primarily known for international flights, Zanzibar International Airport also serves as a crucial hub for domestic travel. It's located near Stone Town, the capital of Zanzibar, making it accessible for both international and domestic connections.

2. **Abeid Amani Karume International Airport (PMA):** Located in Pemba, a smaller island within the Zanzibar Archipelago, this airport serves as the main gateway to Pemba Island. Travelers arriving in Pemba can access a range of domestic flights to explore the island further.

Airlines and Destinations

Several domestic airlines operate within Zanzibar, connecting travelers to various destinations on the island. The major airlines providing domestic flights include:

1. **Coastal Aviation:** Coastal Aviation offers an extensive network of domestic flights connecting Zanzibar to other key destinations within Tanzania. These flights provide access to remote and pristine areas of the island.

2. **Auric Air:** Auric Air operates flights within Zanzibar, with a focus on ensuring passengers reach their desired destinations safely and comfortably. Their services cater to travelers looking to explore different parts of the island.

3. **ZanAir:** ZanAir specializes in domestic flights, particularly those connecting Zanzibar with its surrounding islands like Pemba and Mafia. This airline offers a convenient way to explore the Zanzibar Archipelago.

4. Flightlink: Flightlink provides a reliable domestic flight service, linking Zanzibar with various destinations on the Tanzanian mainland. These flights are especially useful if you wish to explore the broader Tanzanian region.

Advantages of Domestic Flights in Zanzibar

1. **Time-Saving:** Domestic flights save you valuable time, particularly if you're moving between Zanzibar's main island and its outer islands. What might be a lengthy road or ferry journey can be reduced to a short flight.

2. **Comfort:** Domestic flights offer comfort and convenience, with modern aircraft and professional service. You can enjoy a smooth and pleasant journey to your chosen destination.

3. **Accessibility:** Zanzibar's terrain can be challenging to navigate by road in some areas. Domestic flights ensure you can access even the most remote and secluded spots on the island.

4. **Island Hopping:** If you're interested in exploring different islands within the Zanzibar Archipelago, domestic flights are the quickest and most efficient way to hop between them.

Booking Domestic Flights

Booking domestic flights in Zanzibar is relatively straightforward. You can reserve your tickets through the official websites of the domestic airlines or via travel agencies. It's advisable to book in advance, especially during peak tourist seasons, to secure your desired flight times and destinations.

Travel Tips for Domestic Flights

- **Baggage Allowance:** Be aware of baggage restrictions, as domestic flights may have different baggage policies than international ones.
- **Arrival Times:** Arrive at the airport well in advance of your domestic flight, typically at least 1 to 2 hours before departure.
- **Weather Considerations:** Weather conditions, especially during the rainy season, can affect flight schedules. Be prepared for potential delays and schedule adjustments.
- **Seating Preferences:** If you have specific seating preferences, such as a window seat for scenic views, make your request during the booking process or at check-in.

Domestic flights in Zanzibar are a convenient and efficient way to explore this beautiful island and its surrounding regions. If you're seeking adventure in remote areas, relaxation on pristine beaches, or cultural experiences in historic towns, these flights provide easy access to the many wonders of Zanzibar.

In conclusion, knowing how to get to Zanzibar and navigating the island's various transportation options will help you make the most of your trip to this tropical paradise.

CHAPTER THREE

ACCOMMODATION OPTION IN ZANZIBAR

Zanzibar offers a diverse range of accommodation options to suit every traveler's preferences and budget. Whether you're looking for luxurious beachfront resorts, cozy guesthouses, or the flexibility of vacation rentals, Zanzibar has it all. Below, we've provided an overview of the types of accommodation you can expect to find on this enchanting island.

Hotels and Resorts

When it comes to accommodation in Zanzibar, the island pulls out all the stops in the realm of luxury. Zanzibar's hotels and resorts epitomize opulence, offering a blend of modern comfort and traditional Swahili charm that ensures a truly unforgettable stay.

Unparalleled Beachfront Bliss: Zanzibar's most prestigious hotels and resorts are strategically placed along the island's idyllic white-sand beaches. These exclusive establishments offer an immersive experience where every moment feels like a dream. Picture yourself waking up to the sound of gentle waves lapping at your doorstep and stepping onto your private terrace with panoramic views of the turquoise Indian Ocean.

Impeccable Service: What sets these accommodations apart is not just their breathtaking locations but also their dedication to providing world-class service. Expect personalized butler service, gourmet dining options, and spa facilities that transport you to a world of relaxation and rejuvenation.

Cultural Elegance: Many of these luxury properties seamlessly blend modern amenities with the island's rich cultural heritage. You'll find Swahili architecture and design elements incorporated into the resort's layout, creating an ambiance that reflects the essence of Zanzibar.

Notable Luxury Resorts: Consider indulging in the lavish offerings of Baraza Resort & Spa, a five-star gem renowned for its opulent villas and top-notch wellness treatments. Alternatively, Zuri Zanzibar captivates guests with its eco-friendly design and superb cuisine. For those who crave a more secluded retreat, The Residence Zanzibar is nestled amidst a lush forest on the southwest coast.

Mid-Range Comfort

Travelers seeking an upscale experience without the extravagant price tag will find a plethora of mid-range hotels and boutique resorts. These accommodations offer a balance between comfort, affordability, and quality.

Beautiful Grounds: Mid-range options often feature stunning tropical gardens, inviting swimming pools, and private beach access. You'll have the opportunity to enjoy the island's natural beauty while still having access to modern conveniences.

Local Flair: Many of these establishments incorporate elements of Zanzibari culture into their decor and cuisine, creating a unique and immersive experience. You might find yourself dining under the stars in an open-air restaurant or relaxing in a traditional Swahili lounge.

Recommended Mid-Range Options: Bluebay Beach Resort & Spa is a popular choice with its beautiful beachfront location and diverse dining options. Diamonds La Gemma dell'Est on the northwest coast boasts a stunning setting and offers all-inclusive packages. Uroa Bay Beach Resort, located on the east coast, provides a cozy and welcoming atmosphere.

When choosing a hotel or resort in Zanzibar, it's advisable to book well in advance, particularly during peak tourist seasons. These establishments tend to fill up quickly, so securing your spot ensures a hassle-free and memorable stay on this exquisite island. Whether you opt for the ultimate luxury experience or the comfort of a mid-range resort, Zanzibar's hotels and resorts promise a slice of paradise by the Indian Ocean.

Guesthouses and Hostels

Zanzibar offers a wide range of guesthouses and hostels, catering to various preferences and budgets. If you're a budget-conscious traveler looking for affordable stays or someone seeking a more immersive experience in the local culture, Zanzibar's guesthouses and hostels have you covered. Below, we'll provide you with an overview of these types of accommodations on this captivating island.

Budget-Friendly Stays

Zanzibar is known for its charming guesthouses and hostels, especially in Stone Town and other towns across the island. These options provide a budget-friendly way to experience the authentic side of Zanzibar. Staying in a guesthouse often means enjoying a warm and personal touch, as many are family-run. These properties may not offer all the amenities of a resort, but they compensate with genuine hospitality. Notable guesthouses include Warere Town House and Tausi Palace Hotel

Hostel

For solo travelers, backpackers, or those looking to meet fellow adventurers, hostels are a fantastic choice. They typically offer dormitory-style accommodations and communal spaces where guests can socialize and swap travel stories. Zanzibar's hostels are known for their laid-back atmosphere and affordability. Popular choices include Paje by Night, Lost & Found Zanzibar, and Jambo Brothers Hostel.

Immersion in Local Culture: Choosing a guesthouse or hostel often means immersing yourself in Zanzibar's local culture. Many of these accommodations are nestled within historic buildings or traditional Swahili homes, providing a unique and authentic experience. You'll have the chance to interact with locals, sample homemade cuisine, and gain insights into Zanzibar's rich traditions.

Personalized Experiences: Guesthouses and hostels tend to offer personalized service. Hosts are often keen to assist guests in planning activities and excursions, making your stay even more enjoyable. Plus, the smaller size of these accommodations fosters a sense of community among guests, creating lasting memories and friendships.

When booking a guesthouse or hostel in Zanzibar, it's advisable to do so well in advance, especially if you plan to visit during the peak tourist seasons (June to September and December to January). Prices can vary depending on the time of year, so be sure to plan accordingly. Also, some smaller accommodations may not provide 24-hour reception services, so communicating your arrival time in advance will ensure a smooth check-in process.

Regardless of your choice between a guesthouse or hostel, you'll be treated to Zanzibar's renowned hospitality and the opportunity to explore the island's hidden gems, ensuring a truly memorable stay on this tropical paradise.

Airbnb and Vacation Rentals

For travelers seeking a more personalized and flexible stay in Zanzibar, Airbnb and vacation rentals provide a unique and immersive experience. These options allow you to live like a local, offering a sense of authenticity that traditional hotels may not provide.

A Home Away from Home: Zanzibar's Airbnb listings encompass a wide range of properties, from charming beachfront cottages to cozy apartments in Stone Town's historic alleys. Vacation rentals include villas, bungalows, and even treehouses, providing a diverse array of choices to suit different preferences and group sizes.

One of the primary advantages of Airbnb and vacation rentals is the opportunity to connect with local hosts. They often go the extra mile to ensure your stay is memorable, offering insider tips on the best places to eat, hidden beaches to explore, and cultural experiences to enjoy.

Privacy and Space: Vacation rentals provide a level of privacy and space that's especially appealing to families, groups of friends, or honeymooners. Many properties come equipped with private pools, gardens, and kitchens, allowing you to enjoy a more secluded and self-sufficient holiday.

Cost-Effective for Groups: If you're traveling with a larger group, vacation rentals can be more cost-effective than booking multiple hotel rooms. Sharing a villa or beachfront house can significantly reduce your accommodation expenses while creating lasting memories together.

Local Flavors: Staying in an Airbnb or vacation rental often means you have access to a kitchen. This is fantastic for those who enjoy cooking or want to taste local ingredients. You can shop at local markets and try your hand at preparing some Swahili or international dishes.

Booking and Communication

The process of booking an Airbnb or vacation rental is straightforward. Airbnb, in particular, offers a user-friendly platform for browsing, booking, and communicating with hosts. Payment is secure, and you can read reviews from previous guests to ensure a reliable experience.

Considerations: It's crucial to read property descriptions carefully, taking note of amenities, location, and house rules. Some vacation rentals may have minimum stay requirements, and the cancellation policies can vary. Additionally, communication with hosts is essential, so don't hesitate to ask questions or request additional information before booking.

Advance Planning: Like hotels, popular Airbnb and vacation rental properties in Zanzibar can book up quickly, especially during peak travel seasons. To secure your ideal accommodation, it's advisable to make reservations well in advance.

Ultimately, Airbnb and vacation rentals in Zanzibar offer the opportunity to live your dream island vacation on your terms, enjoying a comfortable and unique home base while you explore the breathtaking beauty and vibrant culture of this Indian Ocean paradise.

CHAPTER FOUR

SIGHTSEEING AND ACTIVITIES

Zanzibar offers a plethora of captivating sights and activities that will leave you enchanted by its natural beauty and rich culture. Whether you're an adventurer, history enthusiast, or simply seeking relaxation, Zanzibar has something for everyone.

Exploring Stone Town

When you set foot in Stone Town, the historic heart of Zanzibar, you step into a world where time seems to have stood still. This UNESCO World Heritage Site is a mesmerizing labyrinth of narrow winding streets, historic architecture, and a vibrant cultural tapestry that reflects centuries of trade and influence from Arabia, India, and Europe.

Forodhani Gardens

Nestled along the picturesque waterfront of Stone Town, stands as a captivating embodiment of Zanzibar's cultural and culinary richness. As the sun begins to set, this enchanting square transforms into a sensory wonderland where tastes, sights, and local traditions converge.

As evening falls, Forodhani Gardens metamorphoses into a food lover's paradise. The night market here is renowned for its diverse selection of Zanzibari street food. From the mouthwatering Zanzibar pizza, a savory pancake stuffed with an array of delicious fillings, to succulent seafood skewers grilled over open flames, your taste buds are in for an extraordinary journey. The seafood, often fresh from the nearby Indian Ocean, is a highlight that draws both locals and visitors.

Sunset Splendor: One of the most enchanting aspects of Forodhani Gardens is the backdrop it provides for a mesmerizing sunset. As you indulge in culinary delights, you can savor the breathtaking views of the sun dipping below the horizon, casting hues of orange and pink over the Indian Ocean. It's a moment of sheer magic and tranquility amid the bustling market.

Local Life and Culture: Beyond its culinary appeal, Forodhani Gardens offers a genuine glimpse into the daily life and vibrant culture of Zanzibar. It's a hub of social activity where locals gather to relax, chat, and enjoy the evening breeze. You'll often find musicians and street performers adding to the lively atmosphere, creating an ambiance that's uniquely Zanzibari.

Artisanal Treasures: In addition to the culinary treats, Forodhani Gardens features a variety of stalls selling artisanal goods. You can browse for handmade crafts, jewelry, clothing, and more. It's an excellent place to pick up souvenirs that reflect the island's rich artisanal heritage.

Forodhani Gardens is not just a place to satisfy your taste buds; it's a multi-sensory experience that immerses you in Zanzibar's cultural tapestry. It's a place where the flavors, colors, and traditions of the island come together to create an unforgettable evening that captures the essence of Zanzibar's charm and hospitality.

Cultural and Historical Sites

Stone Town, the heart of Zanzibar's rich history, is replete with cultural and historical treasures that offer a captivating glimpse into the island's past. As you wander through its winding streets, you'll encounter a tapestry of influences from Arabia, India, Persia, and Europe, all interwoven into the fabric of this UNESCO World Heritage Site.

Palace Museum (Beit al-Sahel)

Beit al-Sahel, commonly known as the **Palace Museum**, is an exquisite piece of Zanzibari history. Once the opulent residence of the Sultan of Zanzibar, it stands as a testament to the island's royal legacy. This architectural marvel boasts traditional Swahili design, featuring intricately carved wooden doors and beautiful Arabic calligraphy.

Inside the museum, visitors are treated to a fascinating collection of artifacts, including royal thrones, ceremonial attire, and historical photographs. The museum provides a glimpse into the extravagant lifestyle of the sultans who once ruled Zanzibar. The well-preserved interiors transport you back to a time when Zanzibar was a thriving center of trade and culture.

Anglican Cathedral of Christ

The **Anglican Cathedral of Christ**, with its stunning Gothic architecture, stands as a solemn reminder of Zanzibar's painful history in the transatlantic slave trade. It was constructed on the site of what was once the largest slave market in East Africa. The altar of the cathedral now occupies the very spot where the market's whipping post stood.

The cathedral's interior is both solemn and awe-inspiring. It's adorned with impressive stained glass windows and a wooden crucifix made from the timbers of a slave ship. Adjacent to the cathedral is the **Slave Memorial**, where visitors can pay their respects to the countless individuals whose lives were affected by the horrors of the slave trade. This site is a poignant testament to Zanzibar's role in the fight against slavery.

Darajani Market

Darajani Market is the vibrant heart of Stone Town's daily life. This bustling market is where Zanzibari residents shop for fresh produce, spices, meats, and everyday necessities. Exploring Darajani Market is a sensory journey - the air is filled with the aroma of spices, and the colorful displays of fruits and vegetables create a visual feast.

Engaging with the friendly vendors is an opportunity to connect with the local culture. Try local snacks, such as samosas and sugarcane juice, and marvel at the variety of spices on offer. It's a sensory adventure that provides a window into the everyday life of the island's residents.

Shangani Area

The **Shangani area** is a vibrant and contemporary neighborhood within Stone Town. Its streets are adorned with striking street art and colorful buildings, creating a lively atmosphere that's perfect for exploration. This district is a fusion of traditional and modern Zanzibari culture.

As you wander through Shangani, you'll encounter a mix of boutiques, cafes, and art galleries. The neighborhood often hosts impromptu street performances and cultural events, making it a hub of local creativity and expression. It's a great place to soak in the island's contemporary cultural scene.

Maruhubi Palace Ruins

Hidden away on Zanzibar's lush east coast, the **Maruhubi Palace Ruins** offer a glimpse into the island's royal history. This once-grand palace was a retreat for sultans and their consorts, showcasing the opulence of the time. Today, the ruins are overgrown with vegetation, lending an air of mystery to the site.

Exploring the palace grounds, you'll come across the remains of ornate baths and courtyards. The crumbling walls and arches hint at the grandeur that once characterized this royal residence. It's a tranquil place to reflect on Zanzibar's historical splendor amid the serenity of nature.

Livingstone House

Named after the renowned Scottish explorer Dr. David Livingstone, **Livingstone House** is a charming historical site. Dr. Livingstone stayed in this house during his time in Zanzibar while preparing for his African expeditions. The house itself is a fine example of the architecture of the colonial era, with its graceful verandas and high ceilings.

Today, Livingstone House contains a small museum dedicated to the explorer's life and travels. Visitors can peruse exhibits showcasing his expeditions and the impact of his explorations on the world. The house and museum provide a glimpse into the life of a man who left an indelible mark on the history of exploration.

Overall, exploring these cultural and historical sites in Stone Town is like stepping into a living history book. Each site tells a story of Zanzibar's multifaceted past, from the opulence of the sultans to the resilience of those who fought against the injustices of the slave trade. Whether you're a history enthusiast or simply seeking a deeper understanding of Zanzibar's rich heritage, these sites will leave you both informed and inspired.

Relaxing On the Beaches

Zanzibar's pristine beaches are the epitome of tropical paradise, with powdery white sands and azure waters that stretch as far as the eye can see. Whether you're a sun worshipper, an adventurer, or a romantic at heart, Zanzibar's beaches offer something for everyone.

Nungwi Beach
Location: Northern tip of Zanzibar Island

Nungwi Beach, situated at the northern tip of Zanzibar Island, is a quintessential tropical paradise renowned for its pristine shores and vibrant atmosphere. If you're a sun seeker, water sports enthusiast, or simply in search of relaxation, Nungwi Beach has something to offer every traveler.

Nungwi Beach boasts a long stretch of powdery white sand framed by lush palm trees and the clear, turquoise waters of the Indian Ocean. Here's what you can enjoy:

- **Sunbathing**: The soft, inviting sands provide the perfect spot for sunbathing. Whether you're lounging on a beach towel or relaxing on a sunbed, the warm tropical sun and gentle sea breeze make it a haven for relaxation.

- **Swimming**: The waters at Nungwi are calm and inviting, suitable for swimmers of all levels. The gradual slope into the sea ensures a safe and enjoyable experience.

- **Water Sports**: Thrill-seekers can choose from an array of water sports, including jet skiing, parasailing, paddleboarding, and kayaking. The warm waters and reliable ocean breezes make Nungwi a water sports enthusiast's dream.

- **Traditional Dhow Cruises**: Embark on a traditional dhow boat cruise to explore the coastline, discover hidden coves, and witness the mesmerizing sunset over the Indian Ocean.

- **Deep-Sea Fishing**: Nungwi is renowned for its deep-sea fishing opportunities. Charter a fishing boat and try your luck at catching game fish like marlin and sailfish.

- **Dolphin Watching**: Take a boat tour to see dolphins in their natural habitat. These playful creatures often swim alongside the boats, creating an enchanting experience.

Vibrant Nightlife

As the day transitions into night, Nungwi Beach transforms into a hub of activity and entertainment:

- **Beachfront Bars and Restaurants**: Nungwi boasts a lively dining and nightlife scene. Beachfront bars and restaurants serve fresh seafood, tropical cocktails, and international cuisine. Dining with your toes in the sand under the starry sky is a magical experience.

- **Full-Moon Parties**: If you're lucky enough to visit during a full moon, don't miss the legendary full-moon parties. Dance to the rhythm of local and international beats while enjoying fire dancers and a lively atmosphere.

- **Live Music**: Some beachfront venues offer live music performances, including traditional Taarab music, providing a taste of Zanzibar's rich musical heritage.

Practical Tips

- **Sun Protection**: The sun can be intense; be sure to bring sunscreen, sunglasses, and a wide-brimmed hat to protect yourself.

- **Water Shoes**: While the shoreline is generally sandy, some areas have rocks or coral, so water shoes can be handy.

- **Cash**: Bring enough cash, as not all establishments accept cards.

- **Respect Local Customs**: While the atmosphere is relaxed, remember that Zanzibar is a conservative society. Dress modestly when away from the beach.

Overall, Nungwi Beach in Zanzibar is the epitome of tropical bliss, offering a harmonious blend of relaxation and excitement. Whether you're seeking adventure on the water, vibrant nightlife, or tranquil moments by the sea, Nungwi has it all. This northern paradise is a must-visit destination for any traveler exploring Zanzibar's coastal wonders.

Kendwa Beach

Location: Northwestern Coast of Zanzibar Island

If you're looking for a tranquil and idyllic escape on the island of Zanzibar, Kendwa Beach is your paradise. This pristine stretch of coastline, situated adjacent to the livelier Nungwi Beach, offers a serene and unspoiled atmosphere that is perfect for those seeking relaxation and natural beauty.

Unparalleled Relaxation

Kendwa Beach is a haven for travelers seeking pure relaxation. Here, you can:

- **Laze on the Beach**: The soft, powdery sands of Kendwa are ideal for sunbathing and taking leisurely walks. You'll find it easy to lose track of time as you unwind under the tropical sun.

- **Hammock Haven**: Many beachfront accommodations provide hammocks, inviting you to sway gently while enjoying the sea breeze and the sound of the waves. It's the perfect spot to lose yourself in a good book or simply daydream.

- **Secluded Vibes**: Compared to some of the busier beaches on the island, Kendwa maintains a sense of seclusion and tranquility. The absence of crowds allows you to fully immerse yourself in the serenity of this coastal gem.

Natural Beauty and Activities

While Kendwa Beach is known for its laid-back ambiance, there are still plenty of activities to keep you engaged:

- **Sunset Bliss**: Kendwa Beach offers some of the most breathtaking sunsets on the island. As the sun dips below the horizon, the sky is painted in a symphony of colors, creating a romantic setting that's perfect for couples.

- **Water Activities**: Despite its tranquil vibe, Kendwa Beach is an excellent place for snorkeling and kayaking. The clear, shallow waters make it easy to explore the underwater world, teeming with colorful marine life.

- **Local Encounters**: The village of Kendwa is nearby, offering a chance to interact with friendly locals and experience Zanzibari culture. You may even get the opportunity to witness traditional fishing methods.

- **Beach Volleyball**: Join in or watch friendly games of beach volleyball, a popular activity on Kendwa Beach. It's a great way to socialize with fellow travelers or even challenge some locals to a match.

- **Nighttime Tranquility**: As the day transitions into night, Kendwa retains its peaceful atmosphere. There are no loud beach parties here, making it an ideal spot for stargazing or simply enjoying the calming sound of the waves.

Dining by the Sea

Kendwa Beach offers a selection of charming beachfront restaurants and bars where you can savor freshly caught seafood and other delicious meals with your toes in the sand. The ambiance is relaxed, and the food is often accompanied by the rhythmic tunes of local musicians.

Whether you're a couple seeking a romantic getaway, a solo traveler in search of peace, or a group of friends looking for a quieter beach experience, Kendwa Beach delivers.

Paje Beach
Location: Southeastern coast of Zanzibar Island

Paje Beach is a picturesque haven on the southeastern coast of Zanzibar, known for its unique blend of natural beauty and water sports excitement. Here's a closer look at what you can expect:

- **Kite Surfing**: Paje Beach is celebrated worldwide as a kite surfer's paradise. The consistent trade winds and the shallow Paje Lagoon create ideal conditions for both beginners and experienced kite surfers. There are several kite surfing schools along the beach offering lessons and equipment rental. Watching colorful kites dance across the horizon is a captivating sight.

- **Beachcombing**: The long, expansive beach of Paje invites you to take leisurely strolls along the shore. It's an excellent place for collecting seashells and observing local fishermen at work. During low tide, the ocean retreats, revealing vast sandbars that stretch out to the horizon. This phenomenon provides a unique opportunity for long walks and beachcombing.

- **Coral Rock Pools**: At low tide, you can explore the intriguing coral rock pools that form along the shoreline. These natural pools are teeming with marine life, making them perfect for a bit of snorkeling or simply admiring the colorful fish and sea creatures that inhabit them. It's a fascinating underwater world waiting to be discovered.

- **Beachfront Bars**: When you need a break from all the activities, Paje Beach offers a variety of beachfront bars and restaurants. You can relax in the shade of swaying palm trees, sip on refreshing coconut water, or indulge in a fresh seafood feast while gazing out at the Indian Ocean. It's a perfect way to unwind and soak up the beach vibes.

Paje Beach's unique combination of thrilling water sports, stunning natural beauty, and laid-back beachfront ambiance makes it a must-visit destination for those looking for adventure and relaxation in equal measure.

Jambiani Beach
Location: Southeastern coast, near Paje

Jambiani Beach, located just a short distance from Paje, offers a quieter and more culturally immersive experience. Here's what you can explore at Jambiani Beach:

- **Swim and Sunbathe**: The gentle waves and golden sands of Jambiani Beach create an idyllic setting for swimming and sunbathing. It's a place where you can unwind and enjoy the sun in a less crowded environment compared to some of the more popular beaches on the island.

- **Cultural Experiences**: Jambiani is home to traditional fishing villages, giving you the opportunity to immerse yourself in the local culture. You can interact with friendly villagers, learn about their way of life, and even participate in Swahili cooking classes. It's a chance to gain insight into the rich cultural tapestry of Zanzibar.

- **Kite Flying**: Thanks to the constant breeze, Jambiani is an excellent place for flying kites. You can bring your own kite or purchase one from local vendors. It's a fun and leisurely activity that both adults and children can enjoy.

- **Low Tide Walks**: During low tide, Jambiani Beach reveals an entirely different landscape. Vast sandbars, tidal pools, and unique marine life become visible, creating a serene and almost meditative atmosphere. It's an excellent

- opportunity for long walks along the beach and exploration.
- **Local Artisans**: Support local artisans and shop for handcrafted souvenirs. You'll find an array of items such as intricately woven baskets, colorful kikoys (sarongs), and other handmade crafts. Purchasing these items not only provides you with unique keepsakes but also contributes to the livelihoods of the talented local craftsmen.

Jambiani Beach offers a more tranquil and authentic Zanzibari experience. It's the place to slow down, connect with the local community, and appreciate the simplicity and beauty of the island's southeastern coast.

Spice Plantations

Zanzibar's Spice Plantations are a fragrant and educational delight, offering visitors a chance to explore the island's rich agricultural heritage and the origins of its nickname, the "Spice Island." A visit to these plantations is like stepping into a living spice cabinet where you can see, smell, and taste exotic spices in their natural habitat.

Why Visit Spice Plantations in Zanzibar?

1. **Educational Experience**: Spice tours provide a fascinating opportunity to learn about the cultivation, harvesting, and processing of various

spices. Knowledgeable guides explain the history and uses of each spice, offering insights into Zanzibar's agricultural traditions.

2. **Sensory Adventure**: Prepare to awaken your senses as you stroll through the lush plantations. Inhale the intoxicating scents of cloves, cinnamon, cardamom, nutmeg, and vanilla. Feel the textures of different leaves and barks, and taste the spices straight from the source.

3. **Cultural Insight**: Spice farming is deeply intertwined with Zanzibar's history and culture. Discover how these aromatic treasures played a vital role in the island's trade and cultural exchange with the world.

Popular Spice Plantations to Explore

1. The Spice Tour in Stone Town

Begin your spice exploration right in Stone Town with a guided tour of a local spice farm. This introductory tour allows you to experience the spices without venturing far from the city. Learn about the spices, their uses in Zanzibari cuisine, and witness the fascinating process of spice harvesting.

2. Tangawizi Spice Farm

Located in the village of Tangawizi, this family-owned farm offers a more immersive experience. You'll have the chance to touch, smell, and taste a wide variety of spices, and also enjoy a traditional Swahili lunch prepared with freshly harvested ingredients.

3. Kidichi Spice Farm

Kidichi Spice Farm, near Stone Town, offers a glimpse into the island's history as a major spice producer. Explore the fragrant gardens, see the old Persian baths, and sample spices while hearing captivating stories from the knowledgeable guides.

4. Kizimbani Spice Farm

Located in the heart of Zanzibar's spice-growing region, Kizimbani Spice Farm provides an in-depth look at the cultivation of cloves, nutmeg, and other spices. You'll be amazed by the intricacies of spice farming and the care that goes into nurturing these valuable crops.

What to Expect on a Spice tour

- **Guided Tours**: Expect informative guided tours conducted by locals who have a deep connection to the land and its spices. They'll share their knowledge with enthusiasm.
- **Spice Tasting**: Enjoy tasting sessions where you can sample various spices in their raw and processed forms. Be prepared for some taste sensations you've never experienced before.

- **Cooking Demonstrations**: Some tours include cooking demonstrations, showing you how to incorporate the spices into traditional Zanzibari dishes. You might even get to participate in the cooking process.

- **Souvenir Shopping**: Most tours offer the opportunity to purchase fresh spices, essential oils, and other handmade products. These make for wonderful, aromatic souvenirs to take home.

- **Natural Beauty**: Beyond the spices, you'll often find beautiful tropical gardens with an array of other plants and fruits, making for a visually pleasing and peaceful environment.

Visiting Zanzibar's Spice Plantations is not only an educational experience but also a sensory journey through the heart of the island's history and culture. Don't miss the chance to explore these aromatic treasures during your Zanzibar adventure.

Jozani Chwaka Bay National Park

Nestled in the heart of Zanzibar, Jozani Chwaka Bay National Park is a captivating haven of biodiversity and natural beauty. This national park, spanning approximately 50 square kilometers, offers visitors a chance to immerse themselves in the lush landscapes and discover unique wildlife, most notably the rare and endemic red colobus monkey.

Red Colobus Monkeys: The park is famous for being the only place on Earth where you can encounter the Zanzibar red colobus monkey. These striking primates, with their distinctive rusty-red fur and long tails, are a true conservation success story. At Jozani, you have a high chance of observing these charming creatures up close as they swing from tree to tree.

Mangrove Ecosystems: A significant portion of the park consists of mangrove forests, making it a crucial ecological site. Guided walking tours lead you through winding boardwalks, allowing you to explore these unique ecosystems while learning about their importance in protecting coastal areas from erosion.

Birdlife: Jozani Chwaka Bay National Park is a birdwatcher's paradise. Keep an eye out for colorful and diverse bird species, including kingfishers, sunbirds, and the elusive fish eagle. The park's tranquil surroundings provide an excellent backdrop for birdwatching.

Butterflies and Reptiles: As you wander through the forested trails, you'll encounter a variety of butterflies fluttering among the trees. Additionally, the park is home to reptiles like chameleons and colorful agama lizards, adding to the area's rich biodiversity.

Guided Tours

To fully appreciate the park's beauty and wildlife, it's advisable to embark on a guided tour. Knowledgeable guides will share insights about the flora and fauna, as well as the conservation efforts in place to protect the red colobus monkey population. They'll also ensure you have the best chances of spotting these remarkable primates.

Jozani Chwaka Bay National Park plays a pivotal role in the conservation of the red colobus monkey, which is listed as endangered. The park's efforts include habitat preservation, research, and community involvement. By visiting the park, you contribute to these important conservation initiatives.

Practical Information

- **Entrance Fees**: There is an entrance fee to access the park, with proceeds contributing to its conservation.

- **Visiting Hours**: The park is typically open during daylight hours, and guided tours are available throughout the day.

- **Accessibility**: Trails are well-maintained, but some areas may be muddy, so wearing appropriate footwear is recommended.

- **Photography**: Capture the beauty of the park but be mindful not to disturb the wildlife with flash photography.

- **Respect for Nature**: While enjoying the park, remember to leave no trace and respect the natural environment and its inhabitants.

Jozani Chwaka Bay National Park offers a serene and educational escape into Zanzibar's natural wonders. Whether you're an avid nature enthusiast or simply seeking a peaceful retreat, this national park is a must-visit destination that showcases the island's commitment to preserving its unique biodiversity.

Water Sports

Zanzibar's crystal-clear waters and pristine beaches make it a haven for water sports enthusiasts. It doesn't matter if you're a beginner or an experienced water adventurer, there's a range of activities that allow you to immerse yourself in the aquatic wonders of this island paradise.

Snorkeling and Diving
Snorkeling

Zanzibar is a snorkeler's dream, offering a wealth of underwater beauty just waiting to be explored. The warm, clear waters of the Indian Ocean make it an ideal destination for both novice and experienced snorkelers.

1. **Mnemba Atoll**: Located off Zanzibar's northeast coast, Mnemba Atoll is a world-class snorkeling

destination. The atoll is part of a marine conservation area, ensuring pristine and protected reefs. Here, you can dip beneath the surface and find yourself surrounded by an astonishing diversity of marine life. Schools of colorful fish dance among the corals, and it's common to encounter graceful sea turtles and acrobatic dolphins. Snorkeling at Mnemba Atoll is like exploring an underwater oasis.

2. **Blue Lagoon**: For those new to snorkeling or families with children, the Blue Lagoon on Zanzibar's southeast coast is an excellent choice. The lagoon's calm, shallow waters are a haven for a variety of marine species. Grab your snorkel and mask, and you'll soon find yourself in the midst of a vibrant underwater world. Expect to see clownfish, parrotfish, and anemones, all set against a backdrop of beautiful corals.

3. **Chumbe Island Coral Park**: A short boat ride from Stone Town takes you to Chumbe Island, where the Chumbe Island Coral Park beckons with guided snorkeling tours. The park is a marine sanctuary, and its reefs are meticulously preserved. During your snorkeling excursion, you'll encounter a kaleidoscope of marine life, from brilliantly colored nudibranchs to elusive octopuses. The coral formations are a work of art, showcasing nature's creativity beneath the waves.

Diving

Zanzibar is equally captivating for divers, offering an array of underwater experiences for divers of all levels, from beginners to advanced enthusiasts.

1. **Leven Bank**: If you're an experienced diver seeking exhilaration, Leven Bank is a must-visit site. This offshore reef is known for its strong currents, creating an adrenaline-pumping underwater adventure. Divers here can spot a variety of pelagic species, including sharks, rays, and schools of tuna. The underwater topography, with dramatic drop-offs and swim-throughs, adds to the thrill.

2. **Bawi and Hunga Reefs**: Closer to Stone Town, Bawi and Hunga Reefs are suitable for divers with varying levels of experience. These sites are known for their vibrant coral gardens, home to an array of marine life. Keep an eye out for colorful angelfish, parrotfish, and intriguing macro creatures like ghost pipefish. Diving at Bawi and Hunga Reefs is a visual feast of underwater wonders.

3. **Pange Reef**: Pange Reef is an excellent choice for night diving. As the sun sets, the reef comes alive with nocturnal creatures. Witnessing the underwater world in the soft glow of dive lights is a surreal experience. You may encounter creatures

like cuttlefish, moray eels, and lionfish on the prowl. Night diving at Pange Reef is a chance to see the ocean in a whole new light.

In Zanzibar, whether you prefer the simplicity of snorkeling or the depth of diving, the underwater world is teeming with wonders.

Sailing and Windsurfing
Sailing

Sailing in Zanzibar is a serene and captivating experience. The island's coastal waters, often kissed by gentle breezes, provide an ideal setting for sailors of all skill levels. Here's a more detailed look at what sailing in Zanzibar entails:

- **Traditional Dhows**: The heart of Zanzibar's sailing culture beats with the traditional dhow boats. These graceful vessels, crafted from wood and adorned with large, billowing white sails, are an iconic symbol of the island. Dhows offer a unique and authentic way to explore Zanzibar's coastline.
    - **Scenic Cruises**: One of the most enchanting ways to enjoy a dhow is by taking a scenic cruise. These leisurely journeys allow you to soak in the breathtaking coastal views and the clear, turquoise waters of the Indian

Ocean. As the sun dips below the horizon, the tranquil atmosphere and warm sea breeze create a romantic setting for couples or a peaceful escape for solo travelers.

- **Island Hopping**: Many sailing operators offer day trips to nearby islands, such as Prison Island or Bawe Island. These excursions often include snorkeling stops, giving you the chance to explore vibrant coral reefs and encounter a diverse array of marine life.

Windsurfing

Zanzibar's east coast, particularly the areas of Paje and Jambiani, is a windsurfer's dream come true. The combination of shallow lagoons and consistent trade winds creates an exceptional environment for windsurfing adventures:

- **Ideal Conditions**: The shallow lagoons along the east coast provide an excellent setting for windsurfing. They offer a comfortable depth for beginners to stand in while learning and practicing their skills. The steady winds create perfect conditions for gliding across the water, making it an attractive destination for both beginners and experienced windsurfers.

- **Windsurfing Schools**: If you're new to windsurfing, don't worry. Numerous water sports centers and windsurfing schools are scattered along the coast. These centers provide professional instruction and equipment rental, ensuring that you can confidently take to the water.

- **Advanced Windsurfing**: For advanced windsurfers, the consistent winds along the east coast allow for thrilling high-speed rides and jumps. The conditions are ideal for practicing tricks and perfecting your windsurfing technique.

In summary, sailing and windsurfing in Zanzibar offer unique opportunities to connect with the island's natural beauty and harness the power of the Indian Ocean.

Kayaking and Paddleboarding
Kayaking

Kayaking in Zanzibar offers a unique perspective of the island's stunning coastline and a tranquil way to connect with its natural beauty. Here are some key details:

- **Scenic Explorations**: Zanzibar's coastline is dotted with hidden coves, pristine beaches, and intriguing mangrove forests. Kayaking allows you to explore these wonders at your own pace. Glide silently through the calm waters, discovering secluded spots that are inaccessible by larger boats.

- **Guided Tours**: Many tour operators and resorts offer guided kayaking tours. These tours often include experienced guides who can lead you to the best spots while providing insights into the local ecology, wildlife, and culture. Chwaka Bay's mangrove forests and Menai Bay's conservation areas are popular kayaking destinations.
- **Mangrove Adventures**: Paddling through the mangrove forests of Chwaka Bay is a unique experience. These dense, saltwater forests serve as nurseries for various marine species and are home to a diverse array of birds. Kayaking through the labyrinthine waterways is not only a scenic adventure but also an opportunity for wildlife enthusiasts and birdwatchers to spot numerous species.
- **Independence**: For more experienced kayakers, Zanzibar's calm waters offer a sense of independence and solitude. Rent a kayak and venture out on your own to explore hidden gems, or embark on a sunrise or sunset kayaking journey for a serene and romantic experience.

Paddleboarding (SUP)

Stand-up paddleboarding, or SUP, is a growing water sport in Zanzibar, with its own set of unique experiences:

- **Easy to Learn**: Paddleboarding is relatively easy to pick up, making it accessible to beginners. Many resorts and water sports centers offer lessons and rental equipment, including stable boards and paddles. In no time, you'll be gliding gracefully over the waters.

- **Scenic Cruises**: Paddleboarding provides an excellent vantage point for appreciating Zanzibar's coastal beauty. You'll have a front-row seat to the stunning seascapes, including coral reefs, sandy beaches, and clear waters. The gentle swaying of the board adds an element of meditation to your journey.

- **Yoga and Fitness**: Some enthusiasts combine paddleboarding with yoga, creating a unique fusion of balance, nature, and tranquility. It's a fantastic way to engage in wellness practices amidst Zanzibar's serene surroundings.

- **Fitness Benefits**: Paddleboarding is not just a leisurely activity; it's a full-body workout that engages your core, balance, and strength. Whether you're casually paddling or doing yoga on the board, you'll feel invigorated and refreshed.

Both kayaking and paddleboarding offer intimate experiences with Zanzibar's coastal beauty, and they cater to various levels of adventure and fitness.

Big Game Fishing

Zanzibar is a renowned destination for big game fishing, offering anglers the opportunity to test their skills and land some of the most prized and powerful fish in the Indian Ocean. Here's what you need to know about this exhilarating water sport:

The Experience

Big game fishing in Zanzibar is not just a sport; it's an adventure. It involves heading out to the deep waters of the Indian Ocean, where you'll cast your lines for some of the ocean's most formidable predators. It's a thrilling experience that combines the excitement of the hunt with the awe of encountering majestic marine creatures.

Prime Fishing Grounds

The waters around Zanzibar are teeming with a variety of big game fish species, making it a prime location for sport fishing. Some of the most sought-after catches include:

- **Marlin**: Both blue and black marlin are known to inhabit these waters. These powerful fish are famous for their acrobatic displays and fierce fights.

- **Sailfish**: Zanzibar is considered one of the world's best destinations for sailfish. These billfish are known for their incredible speed and agility.

- **Tuna**: Yellowfin and dogtooth tuna are abundant in these waters, providing exciting challenges for anglers.

- **Wahoo**: These sleek, fast predators offer a thrilling catch.

The Fishing Season

The best time for big game fishing in Zanzibar typically runs from October to March when the waters are warmer and fish are more active. However, some species, like sailfish, can be found year-round.

Fishing Charters

To enjoy a successful and safe big game fishing experience, it's advisable to book a fishing charter. Numerous operators in Zanzibar offer fully-equipped boats, experienced captains, and knowledgeable crews who know the best spots for specific types of fish. Eamples include ZanziFish Charters, Zanzibar Big Game Fishing, and Blue Horizon Charters

Catch and Release

Many charters in Zanzibar operate on a catch-and-release basis for certain species, especially for marlin and sailfish. This practice ensures the conservation of these magnificent creatures and sustains the sport for future generations.

Equipment and Gear

You don't need to bring your own fishing gear; the fishing charters provide top-quality equipment, including rods, reels, bait, and tackle. Experienced crew members will assist you throughout the process, from setting up your gear to reeling in your catch.

A Memorable Experience

Big game fishing in Zanzibar is not just about the catch; it's about the whole experience. While waiting for that big strike, you'll have the chance to take in the stunning scenery of the open ocean and maybe even spot some dolphins or turtles along the way. The excitement of battling a powerful fish and the sense of accomplishment that comes with it make for unforgettable memories.

Respect for the ocean and its inhabitants is paramount. Responsible fishing practices are encouraged, including adherence to size and bag limits, safe handling of fish, and conservation-minded approaches.

Dolphin Watching

Dolphin Watching in Zanzibar is a mesmerizing and enchanting activity that allows you to witness these intelligent marine creatures in their natural habitat.

Zanzibar's coastal waters are home to various species of dolphins, with the bottlenose dolphin and spinner dolphin being the most commonly encountered.

The Experience

- **Boat Tours**: Dolphin watching excursions typically begin early in the morning when the chances of spotting these marine mammals are at their highest. You'll embark on a boat tour led by experienced local guides who are well-versed in the dolphins' behavior and habitat.

- **Dolphin Species**: While on the tour, keep your eyes peeled for playful pods of bottlenose dolphins and spinner dolphins. These dolphins are known for their acrobatic displays, including leaping out of the water and spinning in the air, which adds a delightful touch to the experience.

- **Swim with the Dolphins**: Some tours offer the opportunity to swim alongside these friendly creatures. Imagine snorkeling in the turquoise waters while dolphins gracefully glide past you. It's a surreal and deeply memorable encounter that provides a profound connection with the marine world.

The Best Time and Spots

- **Kizimkazi**: Kizimkazi, a fishing village on the southern coast of Zanzibar, is one of the most renowned areas for dolphin watching. The village is close to prime dolphin habitats, and the tours often depart from here.

- **Timing**: The best time for dolphin watching is usually in the early morning when the waters are calm, and the dolphins are active. However, keep in mind that dolphin sightings are never guaranteed, as they are wild creatures with their own behaviors and routines.

Responsible Tourism

- **Respect for Wildlife**: When participating in dolphin watching, it's essential to follow responsible tourism practices. Maintain a respectful distance from the dolphins and avoid any actions that could disturb or stress them.

- **Environmental Conservation**: Many tour operators in Zanzibar are committed to sustainable and eco-friendly practices. Choose a reputable company that prioritizes the well-being of the dolphins and the conservation of their habitat.

What to Bring

- **Swimwear**: If you plan to swim with the dolphins, wear your swim attire under your clothing.

- **Sun Protection**: Don't forget sunscreen, sunglasses, and a hat to shield yourself from the sun.
- **Camera**: Bring a waterproof camera or a GoPro to capture these incredible moments.

Dolphin watching in Zanzibar offers a unique and magical opportunity to connect with nature and witness the beauty of these marine creatures in their natural environment. It's an experience that combines excitement, wonder, and a sense of awe, making it a highlight of any trip to this tropical paradise.

Kiteboarding
Kiteboarding in Zanzibar:

Kiteboarding, often referred to as kitesurfing, is a thrilling water sport that has gained immense popularity along the coast of Zanzibar, especially in areas like Paje and Jambiani. Here's an in-depth look at this exciting activity:

Ideal Conditions:

Zanzibar boasts ideal conditions for kiteboarding, making it a prime destination for both beginners and experienced kiteboarders. The key factors that contribute to its popularity include:

- **Consistent Winds**: The island benefits from consistent trade winds, typically blowing from May to October and December to March. These winds provide a steady and reliable breeze, creating the perfect environment for kiteboarding.
- **Expansive Beaches**: The long stretches of sandy beaches along the eastern coast of Zanzibar provide ample space for launching, riding, and landing. This abundance of open water ensures that kiteboarders have plenty of room to practice and enjoy their sport safely.

Kiteboarding Schools and Rentals

For those new to kiteboarding, or even if you're an experienced rider looking to enhance your skills, numerous kiteboarding schools and rental shops are available. These facilities provide comprehensive lessons, equipment rental, and expert guidance. Highly trained instructors ensure that beginners receive proper training in kite control, safety procedures, and board riding techniques. Some popular ones include Uhuru Kite Zanzibar, Zanzibar Kite Paradise and Jambiani Kite Paradise

Advanced Kiteboarding Spots

Zanzibar offers kiteboarders an array of exciting spots to explore:

- **Paje Beach**: Paje is undoubtedly the epicenter of kiteboarding in Zanzibar. With its shallow lagoon and consistent winds, it's an ideal location for both beginners and experts. The flat, waist-deep water near the shore is perfect for those learning to ride and practice tricks, while the deeper waters further out provide a thrilling challenge for advanced riders.
- **Jambiani Beach**: Adjacent to Paje, Jambiani Beach offers similar conditions but with a slightly more tranquil atmosphere. It's a fantastic choice for those looking to escape the crowds while still enjoying excellent kiteboarding opportunities.

Events and Competitions

Zanzibar occasionally hosts kiteboarding events and competitions, attracting enthusiasts from around the world. These events showcase the island's exceptional kiteboarding scene and provide an opportunity for riders to challenge their skills in a competitive environment.

Safety is paramount in kiteboarding. Always adhere to the guidance of experienced instructors and local regulations. It's crucial to respect safety zones, understand right-of-way rules, and maintain proper kite control to ensure a safe and enjoyable experience.

Jet Skiing and Parasailing

Jet skiing is an exciting water sport that combines speed and adrenaline with the breathtaking beauty of Zanzibar's coastline. Here's what you need to know about jet skiing on the island:

- **Rentals and Guided Tours**: Many beachfront resorts and water sports centers offer jet ski rentals and guided tours. It doesn't matter if you're a beginner or an experienced rider, there's an option for you.

- **Safety First**: Safety is a top priority. Before you embark on your jet ski adventure, you'll receive a safety briefing and be provided with the necessary safety equipment, including life jackets. Make sure to follow all safety instructions and guidelines provided by the operator.

- **Exploring the Coast**: Jet skiing allows you to explore Zanzibar's coastline like never before. You can ride along the shores, discovering hidden coves, remote beaches, and picturesque coastal villages. The crystal-clear waters provide a stunning backdrop for your adventure.

- **Adrenaline Rush**: If you're an adrenaline junkie, you can satisfy your need for speed. Feel the wind in your hair as you throttle up and zip across the ocean, performing thrilling maneuvers like sharp turns and jumps. It's an exhilarating experience that offers a unique perspective of the island.

Parasailing

Parasailing is a remarkable water activity that combines the thrill of flight with the tranquility of floating above the sea. Here's what you can expect when parasailing in Zanzibar:

- **Soaring Above the Sea**: Parasailing involves being harnessed to a parachute-like sail that's attached to a speedboat. As the boat accelerates, you'll gradually ascend into the air. Once aloft, you'll experience the sensation of weightlessness as you soar high above the ocean.

- **Breathtaking Views**: From your vantage point in the sky, you'll have a bird's-eye view of Zanzibar's stunning coastline. The turquoise waters, sandy beaches, and lush green landscapes create a picturesque panorama that's perfect for capturing unforgettable photos.

- **Tandem Flights**: Parasailing is often done in tandem, allowing you to share this extraordinary experience with a friend or family member. It's a fantastic way to create lasting memories together.

- **Safe and Controlled**: Parasailing in Zanzibar is conducted under strict safety standards. Experienced operators ensure that all equipment is in top condition, and you'll receive a safety briefing before takeoff. The takeoff and landing are controlled by the boat's crew, making it a safe and enjoyable experience for participants of all ages.

Some popular rental companies include Zanzibar Watersports Hub, Ocean Thrill Zanzibar, and Aquatic Adventures Zanzibar

It doesn't matter if you choose to rev up the engine on a jet ski or gracefully glide above the sea on a parasail, both activities provide an adrenaline rush and panoramic views of Zanzibar's stunning coastline.

In summary, Zanzibar's water sports scene offers a wide spectrum of experiences. With options for all skill levels, you're sure to find your aquatic adventure in this island paradise. But remember to always prioritize safety and adhere to local guidelines for a memorable and secure water sports experience.

CHAPTER FIVE

CUISINE AND DINING

Zanzibar, often referred to as the "Spice Island," boasts not only stunning landscapes but also a rich and diverse culinary heritage. When it comes to Zanzibar, the experience of dining is as rich and diverse as the island itself.

Traditional Zanzibari Dishes

Zanzibar's traditional dishes are a delightful fusion of flavors influenced by Swahili, Arab, Indian, and European culinary traditions.

Biryani: Zanzibar's biryani is a fragrant and flavorful rice dish cooked with an array of spices, meat (often chicken or seafood), and vegetables. It's a true delight for the senses and a staple of Zanzibari cuisine.

Urojo: Known locally as "Zanzibar mix," urojo is a spicy and tangy soup that's a true culinary adventure. It's made with ingredients like chickpeas, potatoes, boiled eggs, and a tamarind-based sauce, creating a unique and vibrant flavor.

Mishkaki: A street food favorite, mishkaki consists of skewers of marinated meat (often beef or chicken) grilled to perfection over an open flame. The tantalizing aroma and succulent taste make it a must-try for food enthusiasts.

Octopus Curry: Zanzibar's coastal location means an abundance of fresh seafood. Octopus curry is a seafood lover's dream, featuring tender octopus cooked in a rich coconut and spice-infused sauce.

Zanzibar Pizza: These savory "pizzas" are a street food sensation. A dough pocket is filled with a variety of ingredients, including meat, cheese, or even Nutella, and then grilled to crispy perfection. It's a delicious and budget-friendly option.

Pilau: Pilau is a fragrant rice dish infused with a medley of spices, creating an aromatic and savory flavor. Often served with a side of tomato and coconut chutney, it's a comfort food staple in Zanzibar.

Kaimati: These deep-fried sweet dumplings are a popular dessert in Zanzibar. They are golden and crispy on the outside, yet soft and sweet on the inside, often drizzled with a sugar syrup for an extra treat.

Matoke: Matoke is a dish made from green bananas cooked in a coconut and tomato sauce. It's a hearty and satisfying option for vegetarians and a testament to the creative use of local ingredients.

Coconut Bean Soup: A creamy and nutritious soup made with coconut milk and a blend of spices, often served with crusty bread. It's a comforting dish that showcases Zanzibar's reliance on coconut in its cuisine.

Boko Boko Hina: This is Zanzibar's answer to a rich and hearty breakfast. It consists of a coconut and cardamom-flavored porridge, often served with fried bread or mandazi, making it a sweet and savory start to the day.

When dining in Zanzibar, be sure to explore these traditional dishes to truly immerse yourself in the island's unique culinary culture. Each bite tells a story of Zanzibar's history, its vibrant spice trade heritage, and the diverse influences that have shaped its delectable cuisine.

Exploring Seafood Delights

Zanzibar's coastline is a treasure trove of seafood delights, and there are several exceptional seafood restaurants that beckon food enthusiasts from around the world. Here's a deeper dive into the world of seafood dining in Zanzibar:

The Rock Restaurant

Nestled on a small rock in the Indian Ocean, The Rock Restaurant offers a dining experience like no other. Accessible by boat or on foot during low tide, this iconic restaurant provides not just a meal but an adventure.

Imagine dining in a charming, rustic setting surrounded by the tranquil sea. The restaurant is renowned for its romantic sunsets and unique, intimate atmosphere.

Cuisine: The Rock specializes in seafood, with a menu featuring an array of fresh catches. From lobster to octopus, the dishes here are infused with Zanzibar's spice and culinary artistry. Don't miss the grilled calamari and catch of the day.

Tide Matters: The restaurant's accessibility is tide-dependent, so be sure to check the tide tables and make a reservation in advance to secure your table during high tide.

Forodhani Night Market

Location: Located in Stone Town, the historic heart of Zanzibar, Forodhani Gardens transforms into a vibrant night market in the evening, becoming a seafood lover's paradise.

Ambiance: Forodhani Night Market is a lively and bustling place, perfect for those who want to immerse themselves in the local street food culture. It's a fantastic spot for people-watching and enjoying the vibrant atmosphere.

Cuisine: At the market, you can sample a wide variety of seafood dishes prepared right before your eyes. From grilled fish to Zanzibari pizza, there's something to please every palate. The seafood here is incredibly fresh, and the flavors are a testament to Zanzibar's rich culinary heritage.

Must-Try: Be sure to try the Zanzibar mix, a spicy seafood soup that's a favorite among locals and tourists alike.

Local Seafood Spots

Apart from these renowned establishments, Zanzibar boasts numerous local seafood restaurants and shacks along its coastline. These hidden gems offer the chance to dine like a local, with your feet in the sand and the scent of the ocean in the air.

The hallmark of these local spots is the freshness of their seafood. You can often handpick your catch of the day, which is then expertly prepared and served with simple yet delicious accompaniments.

Expect a laid-back, island-style atmosphere where you can unwind, enjoy the sea breeze, and feast on the day's catch.

Dining at local seafood spots is often more budget-friendly than the high-end restaurants, making it an excellent option for travelers seeking an authentic experience without breaking the bank.

If you're looking for a romantic, picturesque dinner at The Rock or a vibrant and authentic street food experience at Forodhani Night Market, Zanzibar's seafood dining scene promises a delectable journey through the flavors of the Indian Ocean. Don't forget to pair your meal with a refreshing glass of freshly squeezed juice or a local spiced tea for the complete Zanzibari culinary adventure.

International Cuisine

In addition to its rich local flavors, Zanzibar also boasts a delightful array of international cuisines, reflecting the island's historical influences and cosmopolitan character. Here's a closer look at some of the international culinary experiences you can savor:

Indian Delights: The Indian influence on Zanzibar's cuisine is unmistakable. Explore the tantalizing world of Indian cuisine, from fragrant tandoori dishes to rich, aromatic curries. Whether you're craving butter chicken, tikka masala, or vegetarian biryani, Zanzibar's Indian restaurants serve up these classics with flair.

Italian Pizzerias: If you're in the mood for pizza, Zanzibar's Italian pizzerias will not disappoint. Enjoy thin-crust, wood-fired pizzas topped with a variety of ingredients, from classic Margheritas to exotic seafood combinations. The island's pizzerias bring a taste of Italy to this tropical paradise.

Chinese Eateries: Zanzibar's dining scene extends to Chinese cuisine, with restaurants serving up favorites like sweet and sour chicken, dim sum, and delicious stir-fries. It's a wonderful option for those looking to diversify their palates during their visit.

Continental Fare: For a taste of continental Europe, explore restaurants that offer dishes ranging from French cuisine, with its delicate pastries and sauces, to hearty German sausages and bread. These establishments provide a break from the traditional Zanzibari menu.

Mediterranean Delights: The Mediterranean influence is also evident in Zanzibar's dining options. Savor dishes like falafel, shawarma, and grilled kebabs, often accompanied by fresh salads and creamy tahini sauce.

International Fusion: Zanzibar has its own take on fusion cuisine, blending local ingredients with international flavors. You might encounter unique creations that infuse Swahili spices into international dishes or experiment with seafood in unconventional ways.

International Cafes: Relax in cozy cafes that serve a range of international coffees, pastries, and light meals. Enjoy a cappuccino with a view of the ocean or savor a slice of cake paired with a soothing cup of tea.

Some popular international dining options include **Lukmaan Restaurant, Upendo Zanzibar, Serena Inn Restaurant, La Taverna Restaurant and Kendwa Rocks Restaurant.**

It doesn't matter if you're craving the familiar tastes of home or seeking to expand your culinary horizons, Zanzibar's international cuisine scene has something for every palate. These diverse dining options add another layer to the island's already rich and vibrant food culture, ensuring that every meal is an adventure.

Street Food

Exploring the street food scene in Zanzibar is like embarking on a culinary adventure. Here, you'll find an array of mouthwatering dishes and snacks that not only satisfy your taste buds but also provide a taste of the local culture.

Zanzibar Pizza: Zanzibar Pizza is a unique culinary creation that's beloved by both locals and tourists. It's not your typical pizza; instead, it's more like a savory filled pastry. Vendors start with a circle of dough and then add an assortment of ingredients. You can choose from a variety of fillings, ranging from minced meat, vegetables, cheese, and even sweet options like Nutella and banana. The dough is then expertly folded over the ingredients and cooked on a griddle to create a crispy, flavorful delight. It's a must-try street food item that's as diverse as the people of Zanzibar.

Mandazi: Mandazi is a popular snack in Zanzibar, often enjoyed for breakfast or as a quick bite throughout the day. These deep-fried doughnut-like pastries are mildly sweet and have a delightful hint of coconut and cardamom. They're typically served hot, making them an irresistible treat. Locals love to pair mandazi with a cup of spiced tea, creating a harmonious balance of flavors.

Sugar Cane Juice: As you wander the streets of Zanzibar, you'll likely encounter vendors selling freshly squeezed **sugar cane juice**. This refreshing drink is perfect for quenching your thirst, especially in the warm island climate. The sugar cane is passed through a press to extract its sweet, natural juice, which is then served in a glass or plastic bag with a straw. It's a simple yet satisfying way to hydrate and experience a taste of Zanzibar's agricultural abundance.

Exploring the Street Food Scene

Zanzibar's street food vendors often set up shop in bustling markets, near popular tourist spots, or along the beachfront. Here are some tips for navigating the street food scene:

- **Try Local Specialties**: Don't hesitate to sample dishes that might be unfamiliar. The locals take pride in their culinary traditions, and you might discover a new favorite.

- **Hygiene**: While street food can be delicious, be mindful of hygiene. Look for vendors who follow good food-handling practices, like using clean utensils and washing their hands.

- **Engage with Locals**: Strike up a conversation with the vendors. They are often friendly and eager to share their culinary traditions and stories with curious travelers.

Zanzibar's street food is not just about food; it's an integral part of the island's culture. So, as you explore the streets, take your time, savor the flavors, and relish the unique culinary experiences that Zanzibar's street food vendors have to offer.

Dining Tips

One of the defining features of Zanzibari cuisine is its use of spices. When dining in Zanzibar, embrace the opportunity to savor the rich and aromatic flavors derived from spices such as cinnamon, cloves, cardamom, and vanilla. These spices are not just ingredients; they are a cultural heritage, reflecting the island's historical significance in the global spice trade. So, be adventurous with your palate and try dishes that showcase these spices.

- **Timing Matters:** Zanzibari dining often operates at a different pace. Be prepared for a relaxed dining experience, especially at local restaurants. It's common for dishes to take some time to prepare, so patience is key. However, the wait is well worth it, as you'll be treated to fresh, meticulously crafted meals.
- **Beachfront Dining:** Many restaurants in Zanzibar offer stunning beachfront dining experiences. Whether it's a candlelit dinner on the shore or lunch with your toes in the sand, these beachside settings are both romantic and picturesque. To secure the best spots, consider making reservations, especially during peak tourist seasons.
- **Respect the Culture:** Respect for local customs and traditions is vital. When dining, especially in more conservative areas, dress modestly and be mindful of local customs. For example, it's courteous to ask for permission before taking photos of individuals or their establishments.

By keeping these dining tips in mind, you'll not only enhance your culinary experience in Zanzibar but also show respect for the local culture, making your journey even more enjoyable and enriching.

CHAPTER SIX

SHOPPING IN ZANZIBAR

Zanzibar offers a vibrant and colorful shopping experience that reflects the island's rich cultural diversity. From bustling markets to artisan workshops, there are numerous opportunities to find unique souvenirs and treasures. Here's what you should know about shopping in New Caledonia:

Markets

Zanzibar's markets are vibrant hubs of activity, where you can immerse yourself in the island's culture, sample exotic spices, and find unique souvenirs. Here's an in-depth look at some of the most popular markets in Zanzibar:

Darajani Market

Darajani Market, located in the historic heart of Stone Town, is a sensory extravaganza that epitomizes the essence of Zanzibari culture. This bustling market is a must-visit for travelers looking to immerse themselves in the vibrant tapestry of the island's daily life. Let's explore Darajani Market in detail:

Aroma of Spices: As you approach Darajani Market, your senses are instantly awakened by the enchanting aroma of exotic spices that waft through the air. Zanzibar's reputation as the "Spice Island" is well-deserved, and this market is the epicenter of that legacy. Spice vendors offer a mesmerizing array of cloves, cardamom, cinnamon, nutmeg, and vanilla. The air is filled with the fragrance of these treasures, and you can witness spice traders expertly sorting, weighing, and packaging their fragrant wares.

Fresh Produce Galore: Darajani Market is a cornucopia of fresh produce. Rows upon rows of colorful fruits and vegetables stretch out before you, showcasing the abundance of the island. Pineapples, mangoes, papayas, and bananas compete for attention with exotic fruits like jackfruit and soursop. It's not only a feast for the eyes but an opportunity to taste the tropical flavors of Zanzibar.

Textiles and Kangas: As you navigate through the labyrinthine alleys of the market, you'll come across stalls piled high with textiles and kangas. Kangas are traditional East African sarongs that are often worn by Zanzibari women. They come in a dazzling array of patterns and colors, each with its unique message or proverb. Whether you're looking for a fashionable accessory or a meaningful souvenir, Darajani Market has you covered.

Haggling and Bargaining: A visit to Darajani Market is incomplete without a bit of haggling. Bargaining is a time-honored tradition here, and vendors often expect it.

Engage in friendly negotiations to secure the best deals on spices, textiles, or fresh produce. Remember that haggling is part of the local culture, so enjoy the process while respecting the vendors.

Local Snacks and Street Food: Adjacent to Darajani Market, you'll find a bustling section dedicated to street food. Local vendors whip up delectable Zanzibari snacks such as coconut samosas, sugar cane juice, and grilled maize. It's an excellent opportunity to satisfy your taste buds with authentic flavors and interact with friendly locals.

Cultural Experience: Beyond shopping, a visit to Darajani Market offers a profound cultural experience. You'll encounter a diverse array of people, from traders in traditional attire to tourists seeking culinary adventures. The market is a vibrant microcosm of Zanzibari life, and it's a great place to engage with locals and learn about their traditions.

Pro Tips:

- **Timing**: Darajani Market is most active in the mornings when the fresh produce arrives and the spice stalls are at their aromatic best.

- **Photography**: Feel free to take photos, but always ask for permission before photographing people, as some may prefer not to be captured on camera.

- **Exploration**: Don't be afraid to explore the market's nooks and crannies. Some of the most fascinating discoveries are found off the beaten path.

A visit to Darajani Market is a sensory adventure that will leave an indelible mark on your Zanzibar journey. It's a place where you can taste, smell, and experience the heart and soul of the Spice Island, and it's a must-visit destination for any traveler seeking an authentic cultural immersion.

Forodhani Night Market

The Forodhani Night Market in Stone Town is a vibrant and bustling epicenter of culinary delight. Situated along the picturesque waterfront of Stone Town, this nightly food market has become an iconic attraction for both locals and travelers alike. Here, the air is filled with the enticing aromas of grilled seafood, spices, and Zanzibari street food, creating an atmosphere that's truly one of a kind.

What to Find:

1. **Street Food Extravaganza**: The heart and soul of Forodhani Market is its exceptional array of street food stalls. As the sun sets, the market comes to life with vendors setting up their grills and stoves. Seafood takes center stage, with skewers of fresh

fish, lobster, prawns, and squid sizzling over open flames. It's a seafood lover's paradise, and you can watch as your meal is expertly prepared right in front of you.

2. **Pizza Zanzibari**: One of the most popular items at Forodhani is "Pizza Zanzibari." It's not your typical pizza; it's a unique local twist, where a doughy base is topped with minced meat, vegetables, and a variety of spices. Watching it being cooked on a round griddle is an experience in itself.

3. **Swahili Delicacies**: Explore Swahili cuisine by trying dishes like "Zanzibar Mix," a flavorful blend of spices, fruits, and fried potatoes. You can also sample cassava and sweet potato fries, samosas, and coconut pancakes known as "mkate wa sinia."

4. **Fresh Sugarcane Juice**: Quench your thirst with a glass of fresh sugarcane juice, a popular and refreshing beverage offered by several vendors.

5. **Sweets and Desserts**: Don't forget to satisfy your sweet tooth with Zanzibari sweets. You'll find vendors offering sugary delights like fried doughnuts and coconut ladoos.

Pro Tips:

- **Come Hungry**: The variety of food available can be overwhelming, so arrive with an appetite and be ready to indulge in a gastronomic adventure.

- **Bargaining**: While prices are generally reasonable, bargaining is a common practice. Feel free to negotiate, but do so respectfully.

- **Hygiene**: Look for stalls with clean cooking areas and fresh ingredients to ensure a safe and delicious dining experience.

- **Local Atmosphere**: Forodhani isn't just about food; it's also a social gathering place for locals and tourists alike. Strike up a conversation, enjoy the live music, and soak in the vibrant atmosphere.

- **Evening Hours**: The market comes alive in the evening and is most active after sunset. Plan to visit during these hours to experience Forodhani at its best.

- **Seating**: There are seating areas with benches and tables set up along the seafront. Grab a seat with a view and enjoy your meal with the sound of waves in the background.

The Forodhani Night Market is not merely a place to eat; it's a celebration of Zanzibari culture and cuisine. It offers a sensory journey through the island's flavors, where you can mingle with locals, savor delicious food, and create unforgettable memories against the backdrop of Stone Town's historic waterfront.

Mkokotoni Fish Market

Mkokotoni Fish Market, located in the picturesque village of Nungwi on the northern tip of Zanzibar, is more than just a marketplace; it's a vibrant cultural experience that allows you to immerse yourself in the daily life and traditions of Zanzibar's fishing communities.

Location and Atmosphere

Mkokotoni Fish Market is nestled along the coastline of Nungwi, known for its stunning beaches and clear waters. The market is a true representation of Zanzibari coastal life. It's not a tourist-oriented market, but rather a place where local fishermen, traders, and villagers converge daily, creating a bustling and lively atmosphere.

To fully appreciate the Mkokotoni experience, consider an early morning visit when the market is at its most vibrant. The day begins before sunrise, as local fishermen set out to sea in their traditional wooden dhows, returning later with their morning catch. The market comes to life as the boats approach the shore, and the day's fresh catch is brought ashore.

The Auction Ritual: One of the highlights of Mkokotoni Fish Market is the animated and theatrical fish auctions that take place as soon as the boats dock. This is where you can witness the lively and competitive nature of the fish trade. Fishermen and buyers engage in spirited bidding wars, with the prices fluctuating based on supply and demand. It's a fascinating spectacle and an excellent opportunity to interact with the locals.

Variety of Seafood: While fish are the primary attraction, the market offers a wide variety of seafood. Depending on the day and the season, you might find octopus, crabs, prawns, and even lobsters. The seafood here is incredibly fresh, having just been plucked from the Indian Ocean, making it a prime spot for seafood lovers and home cooks looking for the freshest ingredients.

Engaging with the Locals: One of the most rewarding aspects of visiting Mkokotoni Fish Market is the chance to engage with the local fishermen and traders. They are usually friendly and open to conversations, allowing you to learn about their traditional fishing methods, cultural practices, and daily routines. It's an opportunity to gain a deeper understanding of the local way of life.

Respecting Local Customs: As a visitor, it's essential to respect the local customs and traditions. While photography is generally allowed, always ask for permission before taking someone's picture, and be sensitive to the fact that you are in a working environment. Additionally, dress modestly and be mindful of your behavior.

Buying Fresh Seafood: If you're staying in self-catering accommodation or with access to a kitchen, Mkokotoni Fish Market is an ideal place to purchase fresh seafood. The prices are often competitive, and you can select the exact seafood you want, ensuring top-notch quality for your culinary adventures.

If you're seeking an off-the-beaten-path adventure and a deeper connection with Zanzibar's coastal culture, Mkokotoni Fish Market is a must-visit destination.

Souvenirs

When you visit Zanzibar, you'll undoubtedly want to bring home a piece of this enchanting island as a memento of your journey. Zanzibar offers a delightful array of souvenirs that encapsulate its culture, history, and natural beauty. Here's an in-depth look at the souvenirs you can find in Zanzibar:

When you visit Zanzibar, you'll undoubtedly want to bring home a piece of this enchanting island as a memento of your journey. Zanzibar offers a delightful array of souvenirs that encapsulate its culture, history, and natural beauty. Here's an in-depth look at the souvenirs you can find in Zanzibar:

1. Kangas and Kitenges: Kangas and kitenges are vibrant, colorful pieces of cloth that serve as more than just souvenirs. They are integral to Swahili culture and are often used as garments, head coverings, and even baby carriers. Kangas are adorned with various designs, including Swahili proverbs, floral motifs, and geometric patterns. When you buy a kanga or kitenge, you're taking home a piece of Zanzibari tradition. These textiles are perfect for creating unique clothing, home decor, or framing as wall art.

2. Wooden Carvings: Zanzibar is renowned for its intricate woodwork, which ranges from small figurines to large sculptures and furniture. Local artisans craft these pieces from a variety of indigenous woods like ebony, mahogany, and teak. The carvings often depict traditional Swahili designs, animals, and scenes from daily life. Wooden carvings are not only visually stunning but also a tangible connection to Zanzibar's artistic heritage. Consider purchasing a carving to add a touch of exotic elegance to your living space.

3. Spices: As the "Spice Island," Zanzibar is famous for its aromatic spices like cloves, vanilla, cinnamon, and nutmeg. You can find these spices in local markets and spice plantations. Buying Zanzibari spices allows you to take home the essence of the island's rich history and its contribution to the global spice trade. Look for fresh, high-quality spices and consider packaging them in airtight containers to preserve their fragrance.

4. Jewelry: Zanzibar's jewelry scene is a treasure trove of unique and eye-catching pieces. Local artisans create jewelry using colorful beads, semi-precious stones, and silver. The beadwork often reflects Swahili traditions and features intricate patterns. Silver jewelry showcases traditional Swahili designs and motifs. Purchasing Zanzibari jewelry lets you carry a piece of the island's vibrant culture with you. Whether you opt for a beaded necklace, a silver bracelet, or a pair of Swahili-inspired earrings, these adornments are both fashionable and meaningful.

5. Baskets and Woven Goods: Zanzibar is home to skilled weavers who craft baskets, mats, and bags from natural materials like palm fronds and sisal. These products are not only eco-friendly but also practical and decorative. Baskets and mats are often adorned with colorful patterns and designs. They make excellent souvenirs or functional pieces for your home.

6. Artwork and Paintings: For those who appreciate visual art, Zanzibar offers a thriving art scene. Local artists create a diverse range of paintings, from traditional scenes to contemporary pieces inspired by the island's beauty. Visit galleries and artist workshops in Stone Town to discover unique artwork that captures the essence of Zanzibar. Acquiring a painting or artwork can be a meaningful way to remember your trip.

7. Masks and Traditional Artifacts: Traditional African masks and artifacts are available in various markets and curio shops on the island. These items often carry cultural significance and can be striking decorative pieces or collectors' items. While purchasing masks or traditional artifacts, inquire about their cultural context and meaning, as these pieces have stories to tell.

When shopping for souvenirs in Zanzibar, take your time to explore local markets, artisan workshops, and galleries. Engage with the local artisans and vendors to learn about the significance and craftsmanship behind the items you choose. Each souvenir you select will not only remind you of your journey but also serve as a connection to the rich and diverse culture of Zanzibar.

Arts and Crafts

Zanzibar's arts and crafts scene is a vibrant reflection of the island's rich cultural heritage and creative spirit. When exploring the artistic offerings of Zanzibar, you'll encounter a diverse range of traditional and contemporary creations that tell the stories of the island's history, culture, and its people. Here's a comprehensive look at the world of arts and crafts in Zanzibar:

Maruhubi Arts & Crafts Centre
Location: Maruhubi, Stone Town

Overview: Maruhubi Arts & Crafts Centre, nestled in the heart of Stone Town, stands as a cultural haven where local artists and craftsmen come together to showcase their talents. It's a captivating space filled with creativity and tradition, offering visitors an opportunity to delve into the island's artistic soul.

Craftsmanship:

1. **Paintings**: Explore a mesmerizing collection of paintings that range from traditional Swahili art to contemporary pieces. These paintings often depict scenes from Zanzibar's daily life, historical events, and the island's stunning landscapes.

2. **Sculptures**: The center houses a variety of sculptures crafted from locally sourced materials like wood, stone, and coral. These sculptures often reflect Zanzibar's multicultural influences, blending Swahili, Arab, and African styles.

3. **Handmade Crafts**: Be prepared to be dazzled by a wealth of handmade crafts, including intricately carved wooden items such as masks, furniture, and decorative boxes. These items make for excellent souvenirs, each bearing the mark of Zanzibar's skilled artisans.

Interaction with Artists: One of the unique aspects of Maruhubi Arts & Crafts Centre is the opportunity to engage directly with the artists and craftsmen. You can observe them at work, ask questions, and gain insight into their creative processes. This connection enhances the appreciation of the art and allows you to understand the stories behind the pieces.

Supporting Local Communities: Purchasing items from Maruhubi Arts & Crafts Centre is not just a transaction; it's a contribution to the local economy and the preservation of traditional craftsmanship. Many of the artists and craftsmen here rely on their work to sustain their families and communities.

Zanzibar Curio Shop

The Zanzibar Curio Shop is a conveniently located treasure trove of Zanzibari arts and crafts. Situated in the heart of Stone Town, it offers a wide range of items that capture the essence of the island's culture and history.

Craftsmanship:

1. **Traditional Clothing**: Discover a selection of traditional Zanzibari clothing, including the colorful kangas and kikois that locals often wear. These garments are not only beautiful but also comfortable, making them a popular choice among visitors.

2. **Jewelry**: The shop features an array of jewelry crafted from local beads and semi-precious stones.

You can find intricately designed necklaces, bracelets, and earrings that showcase the artistry of Zanzibar's jewelry makers.

3. **Art Prints**: For those seeking smaller and more portable mementos, the shop offers art prints and postcards featuring Zanzibar's landscapes, architecture, and vibrant street scenes.

Cultural Exploration: Zanzibar Curio Shop allows visitors to immerse themselves in Zanzibar's culture through its offerings. The traditional clothing and jewelry, in particular, offer a chance to experience the island's unique style and flair.

Shopping Tips: When shopping for arts and crafts in Zanzibar, it's essential to be respectful of the local culture and artisans. Bargaining is common in markets and smaller shops, but do so politely. Take your time to browse and choose items that resonate with you, and remember that each piece holds a piece of Zanzibar's cultural mosaic.

Overall exploring the arts and crafts scene in Zanzibar is not just about purchasing beautiful objects; it's about connecting with the island's culture, history, and people. Whether you visit Maruhubi Arts & Crafts Centre for a deeper dive into artistic traditions or the Zanzibar Curio Shop for a convenient and eclectic shopping experience, you're sure to find pieces that capture the essence of this enchanting island and make your trip unforgettable.

CHAPTER SEVEN

NIGHTLIFE IN ZANZIBAR

As the sun sets over this enchanting island, a whole new world comes alive, offering travelers an opportunity to experience the pulsating energy and unique cultural expressions that define Zanzibar's after-dark adventures. In this section, we will be your guide to the captivating nightlife of Zanzibar, where beach parties, live music, and exotic cocktails await your exploration.

Beach Parties

Zanzibar's beach parties are legendary, and for good reason. As the moon rises over the glittering Indian Ocean, the island transforms into a mesmerizing playground of music, dance, and laughter. Here, we delve deeper into what makes these beach parties an unforgettable experience.

The Setting

Imagine soft, powdery sand beneath your feet, the gentle sound of waves caressing the shore, and a star-studded sky overhead. This is the enchanting backdrop of Zanzibar's beach parties. The island's beaches, particularly Nungwi and Kendwa, come alive after dark. Beachfront bars and clubs set up their sound systems right on the sand, creating a seamless transition from daytime relaxation to nighttime revelry.

The heartbeat of these parties is the music. Local and international DJs spin an eclectic mix of tunes, ranging from Afrobeat and reggae to electronic dance music. The rhythmic beats are irresistible, encouraging even the most reserved visitors to hit the dance floor. The ambiance is infectious, drawing people from all corners of the island, creating a melting pot of cultures and energy.

Tropical Libations

No beach party is complete without a tropical cocktail in hand. Sip on freshly mixed mojitos, piña coladas, or the local favorite, 'Dawa.' These drinks not only quench your thirst but also add to the exotic experience. Picture yourself savoring the flavors of Zanzibar while watching the sea shimmer in the moonlight.

To add an extra layer of enchantment, fire dancers often take the stage. These mesmerizing performers twirl flaming poi and create breathtaking patterns in the night sky. Their performances are a visual spectacle that adds to the otherworldly atmosphere of the beach parties.

Zanzibar's beach parties are more than just gatherings; they are communal experiences. Strangers become friends, and the partygoers form a vibrant, united community for the night. It's an opportunity to interact with both locals and fellow travelers, share stories, and create lasting memories.

Timing and Tips

Beach parties typically start in the late evening and can last until the early hours of the morning. Dress comfortably, as the island's warm climate is perfect for dancing the night away in light clothing. Remember to stay hydrated, especially if you're dancing energetically. And while these parties are generally safe, it's always wise to keep an eye on your belongings.

Some popular beach parties include Full Moon Party at Kendwa Rocks, Sunset Party at Nungwi Beach and Jambo Beach Bash in Jambiani

Zanzibar's beach parties are not just about dancing; they're about embracing the island's carefree spirit, celebrating life, and feeling the pulse of the Indian Ocean under a starry sky

Live Music

Zanzibar's live music scene is a treasure trove of diverse musical genres that reflect the island's rich cultural heritage. When the sun sets and the island takes on a different charm, live music becomes the heartbeat of the night. Here's what you can expect:

Taarab Music

Taarab music is the jewel in Zanzibar's musical crown. It's a soul-stirring blend of Swahili, Arab, and Indian influences, accompanied by mesmerizing melodies and poetic lyrics. Listening to Taarab is like taking a journey through Zanzibar's history and culture. You can catch Taarab performances in dedicated venues or sometimes even impromptu gatherings in Stone Town. The intricate rhythms, haunting vocals, and mesmerizing orchestration will leave you spellbound.

Reggae and Afrobeat

Zanzibar's love affair with reggae and Afrobeat is evident in the vibrant live music scene. Local and international bands often jam to these genres in beachfront bars and clubs. The atmosphere is relaxed and the music infectious, making it impossible not to move to the rhythm. Look out for live band performances and DJ sets that fuse these genres with local sounds, creating a unique sonic experience.

Jazz and Fusion

If you're a jazz enthusiast, Zanzibar won't disappoint. Some venues in Stone Town occasionally host jazz performances, showcasing both local and visiting musicians. These intimate settings provide a chance to appreciate the improvisational spirit of jazz while enjoying the island's laid-back vibe.

Where to Experience Live Music

Stone Town is a hub for live music, with venues like the Mercury's Restaurant and Livingstone Beach Restaurant offering regular live performances. However, don't limit yourself to just the town; beachfront bars and resorts across the island often host live bands and DJs. Check with locals or your accommodation for the latest event listings.

Musical Festivals: If your visit coincides with one of Zanzibar's music festivals, such as the Sauti za Busara Festival, consider it a fortunate stroke of fate. These events bring together musicians from across the African continent, creating a melting pot of musical talent that's not to be missed.

Local Talent: Keep an ear out for local street performers too. Zanzibar has a wealth of undiscovered musical talent, and you might stumble upon a mesmerizing performance while wandering the charming streets of Stone Town.

Live music in Zanzibar isn't just about listening; it's about feeling the island's rhythms and connecting with its vibrant culture.

Bars and Clubs

Zanzibar's nightlife scene offers a diverse range of bars and clubs, making it an exciting destination for night owls. If you're in the mood for a quiet drink, live music, or dancing until dawn, Zanzibar has something to suit your taste.

Stone Town's Cozy Bars

Stone Town, with its winding alleys and historic architecture, boasts several intimate bars that offer a welcoming respite from the hustle and bustle of the day. These bars are often small, creating an atmosphere of camaraderie among patrons. Dim lighting, comfortable seating, and tasteful decor create a relaxed ambiance, making them ideal for starting your night on the town.

Local Flavor: One of the joys of visiting Stone Town's bars is the opportunity to sample local drinks. Freshly squeezed sugar cane juice is a refreshing choice, especially on warm Zanzibar evenings. Additionally, you can try freshly brewed spiced tea, a delightful concoction infused with aromatic local spices like cardamom and cloves. These drinks provide a unique taste of Zanzibari culture that you won't want to miss.

Dance Clubs by the Beach

Beachfront Fun: As the sun sets over the Indian Ocean, Zanzibar's beachfront bars transform into vibrant dance clubs. The combination of the cool ocean breeze and the rhythmic music creates a magical atmosphere that's perfect for dancing the night away. DJs often play a mix of international hits and local beats, ensuring that the dance floor is always alive with energy.

Beach Bonfires: Some beach clubs take the beachfront experience a step further by hosting bonfires. Gather around the fire with fellow travelers, and share stories and laughter under the starry Zanzibar sky. It's a memorable way to enjoy the island's nightlife and create lasting memories. "Cholo's Beach Bar" in Nungwi is famous for its beachside bonfires. After dancing the night away, you can gather around a crackling fire, meet fellow travelers, and share stories under the starry Zanzibar sky.

Unique Island Experiences

Full-Moon Parties: If your visit coincides with a full moon, consider attending one of Zanzibar's legendary full-moon parties. These events are known for their energetic and vibrant atmosphere. They are typically held on various beaches around the island, and you can expect fire dancers, glowing decorations, and an eclectic mix of music that keeps the party going until dawn.

Local Hangouts: For a truly authentic experience, venture beyond the tourist hotspots to discover local hangouts. These might be small, unassuming bars where Zanzibaris gather to unwind. While they may not offer an extensive cocktail menu, they provide a genuine glimpse into the island's culture and allow you to mingle with locals and forge connections.

Live Music Fusion: Keep an ear out for live music performances during your night out. Zanzibar's music scene is a fusion of styles, and you might stumble upon a band that combines traditional taarab music with contemporary beats. These performances offer a unique and captivating auditory experience that showcases the island's rich cultural heritage.

Responsible Enjoyment: While Zanzibar is generally safe for tourists, it's important to drink responsibly and be mindful of your surroundings, as you would in any nightlife setting. Traveling with a group is advisable, and it's a good practice to keep an eye on your belongings.

Some popular bars and clubs include Africa House Rooftop Bar, Tatu Bar at Z Hotel and Coral Rock Hotel Bar.

Overall, Zanzibar's bars and clubs cater to a diverse crowd, ensuring that every night out is a memorable experience.

CHAPTER EIGHT

FESTIVALS AND EVENTS

Zanzibar is not only renowned for its stunning natural beauty and historical sites but also for its vibrant and diverse festivals and events that provide a unique opportunity to immerse yourself in the local culture. Here's a comprehensive look at some of the most significant festivals and events you can experience in Zanzibar:

Zanzibar International Film Festival (ZIFF)

JULY, Stone Town

The Zanzibar International Film Festival, often abbreviated as ZIFF, stands as one of the most prominent and culturally enriching events in East Africa. Each July, this festival transforms the historic Stone Town into a hub of cinematic excellence, artistic exploration, and cultural exchange.

ZIFF is celebrated for its commitment to showcasing a diverse array of films. It's a platform where African and international filmmakers converge to present their works. The festival features a range of genres, from thought-provoking documentaries that shed light on important issues facing the continent to entertaining and inspiring feature films.

Nurturing Emerging Talent: One of the festival's core missions is to foster emerging talent in the world of film. ZIFF includes workshops, seminars, and masterclasses conducted by seasoned industry professionals. These sessions offer valuable insights into the art and business of filmmaking, providing aspiring filmmakers with the tools and knowledge they need to succeed.

Cultural Exchange: ZIFF goes beyond cinema; it's a celebration of culture and creativity. In addition to film screenings, you can explore art exhibitions, theater performances, and music showcases. These elements merge to create a holistic experience that allows visitors to immerse themselves in the richness of Zanzibar's cultural tapestry.

The Soko Filamu Market: One of the highlights of ZIFF is the Soko Filamu Market. This marketplace serves as a meeting point for filmmakers, producers, distributors, and investors. It's a space where deals are struck, collaborations are forged, and African cinema gains more recognition on the global stage.

The ZIFF Awards: The festival concludes with the ZIFF Awards ceremony, where outstanding contributions to African cinema are celebrated. Awards are presented in various categories, including Best African Film, Best Director, and Best Documentary. It's a moment of pride for both filmmakers and the African film industry as a whole.

Community Engagement: ZIFF extends its reach beyond Stone Town, organizing screenings and events in other parts of Zanzibar. This community engagement aspect ensures that a broader audience, including local residents, has access to the festival's offerings, contributing to a shared cultural experience.

Preserving Cultural Heritage: ZIFF also plays a crucial role in preserving Zanzibar's cultural heritage. It often screens historical films and documentaries that highlight the island's rich past, including its role in the spice trade and its cultural fusion resulting from centuries of trade and migration.

Social Impact: Beyond the artistic and cultural dimensions, ZIFF is committed to addressing social issues through film. It screens documentaries and feature films that tackle topics like gender equality, environmental conservation, and social justice, sparking important conversations among attendees.

Overall, the Zanzibar International Film Festival is a testament to the power of cinema to educate, entertain, and inspire. It provides a unique opportunity for travelers to not only enjoy world-class films but also immerse themselves in the vibrant cultural scene of Zanzibar while supporting the growth of African cinema.

Sauti za Busara Music Festival

FEBRUARY, Stone Town, Zanzibar

Sauti za Busara, which translates to "Sounds of Wisdom" in Swahili, is a captivating celebration of African music and culture that takes place annually in the historic Stone Town of Zanzibar. This festival has earned a reputation as one of the continent's premier music events, drawing artists, music enthusiasts, and travelers from around the world to the enchanting island of Zanzibar.

Sauti za Busara offers a truly diverse and eclectic musical experience. The festival's main focus is showcasing the rich tapestry of African rhythms and melodies, from traditional sounds rooted in centuries-old traditions to contemporary beats that blend genres and styles.

The festival features musicians from all corners of the African continent, giving attendees the opportunity to explore the musical diversity of this vast and culturally rich continent. Performers come from countries as varied as Mali, Tanzania, Senegal, South Africa, and Kenya, ensuring a truly Pan-African representation.

One of the festival's unique features is the spontaneous and inspiring collaborations that occur between artists from different backgrounds. These collaborations often result in one-of-a-kind performances, uniting artists and audiences in the spirit of musical creativity and unity.

Beyond the Music

While music takes center stage at Sauti za Busara, the festival offers much more than just concerts. Attendees can engage in a range of cultural activities and experiences:

Workshops and Seminars: The festival hosts workshops and seminars that delve into various aspects of African music, including its history, cultural significance, and evolution. Musicians and scholars often lead these discussions, providing valuable insights into the world of African music.

Film Screenings: In addition to live performances, the festival screens documentaries and films related to African music and culture, offering a visual and educational dimension to the event.

Traditional Dance and Art: Traditional African dance troupes and artisans often participate, allowing festival-goers to witness and participate in the vibrant traditions of the continent.

The Spirit of Unity: Sauti za Busara goes beyond the music; it embodies the spirit of unity and cultural exchange. It's a place where people from diverse backgrounds come together to celebrate the beauty and creativity of African culture. The festival promotes a sense of togetherness, breaking down cultural barriers and fostering a sense of global citizenship.

Practical Tips

- **Tickets:** Tickets for the festival are usually available online in advance. It's advisable to purchase them early, as the event attracts a considerable crowd.

- **Accommodation:** Since the festival takes place in Stone Town, there are numerous accommodation options available, from luxury hotels to budget-friendly guesthouses. Booking in advance is recommended, especially during the festival's peak days.

- **Local Cuisine:** Don't miss the opportunity to sample Zanzibar's delicious local cuisine at the festival. From spicy seafood dishes to sweet treats, the culinary offerings are a delightful complement to the music.

Sauti za Busara Music Festival is a captivating journey through the heart of African music and culture. It's an event that celebrates diversity, fosters unity, and leaves a lasting impression on all who attend, making it a must-visit for music lovers and cultural enthusiasts exploring the beautiful island of Zanzibar.

Eid al-Fitr

Eid al-Fitr, also known as **"Eid,"** is one of the most significant and joyous Islamic festivals celebrated in Zanzibar with immense fervor and enthusiasm. This holiday marks the end of **Ramadan,** the holy month of fasting, prayer, and reflection observed by Muslims worldwide. Eid al-Fitr is a time of communal unity, charity, worship, and festive feasting.

Date and Significance: The date of Eid al-Fitr varies each year according to the Islamic lunar calendar. It begins with the sighting of the new moon, which signals the conclusion of Ramadan. In Zanzibar, the exact date is determined by local religious authorities. The holiday holds deep religious and spiritual significance, as it signifies the completion of a month of fasting, self-discipline, and increased devotion to Allah.

Preparation and Festive Atmosphere: In the days leading up to Eid al-Fitr, Zanzibari households bustle with preparations. Homes are thoroughly cleaned and adorned with colorful decorations. Families buy new clothes, often referred to as **"Eid clothes,"** to wear on this special occasion. Markets are bustling with shoppers, and streets are illuminated with decorative lights, creating a festive atmosphere across the island.

Eid Prayers and Sermons: On the morning of Eid, Muslims in Zanzibar gather at mosques, open grounds, and prayer grounds to perform special **Eid prayers.**

These congregational prayers are led by religious leaders and are attended by men, women, and children, all dressed in their finest attire. After the prayers, imams deliver sermons that emphasize the importance of compassion, unity, and gratitude.

Zakat al-Fitr: Before attending the Eid prayers, Muslims in Zanzibar are required to give **Zakat al-Fitr,** a form of charity that is intended to purify those who fast from any indecent act or speech. It is also an opportunity to assist those in need. Zakat al-Fitr ensures that even the less fortunate can participate in the celebrations and enjoy a festive meal.

Feasting and Hospitality: One of the central aspects of Eid al-Fitr in Zanzibar is the elaborate feasting that follows the prayers. Families and friends come together to enjoy a grand meal, which typically includes dishes like **biriani** (spiced rice with meat), **pilau** (spiced rice), various **samosas,** and a variety of sweets like **kashata** (coconut candy) and **mandazi** (deep-fried doughnuts). It's common for neighbors to exchange dishes and visit one another, sharing the joy of the occasion.

Gift Giving: Eid al-Fitr is also a time for giving and receiving gifts. Families exchange presents, particularly children who eagerly anticipate receiving **Eidi,** which are gifts of money or toys. It's a tradition that strengthens familial bonds and spreads happiness among loved ones.

Community Spirit and Charity: Throughout Eid al-Fitr, there is a strong emphasis on charity and helping those less fortunate. Many Zanzibaris participate in community service and donate to charitable organizations. This spirit of generosity extends to providing food to those who may not have enough to celebrate the festival adequately.

For travelers visiting Zanzibar during this auspicious occasion, it's a unique opportunity to witness the island's vibrant Islamic traditions and join in the joyful festivities that mark the end of Ramadan.

Mwaka Kogwa Festival

JULY, Makunduchi Village

The Mwaka Kogwa Festival is a unique and colorful cultural celebration that takes place in Makunduchi Village, located on the southeast coast of Zanzibar. This festival is deeply rooted in Swahili traditions and is celebrated to mark the beginning of the Swahili New Year. It's a four-day event that not only offers visitors a glimpse into Zanzibar's rich heritage but also provides an opportunity to immerse themselves in the local way of life.

Mwaka Kogwa has its roots in Persian and Arab traditions, and its name can be roughly translated to "the dropping of the year." The festival has evolved over centuries, combining elements of different cultures and local customs. It's celebrated with great enthusiasm by the community as it symbolizes the renewal of spirits, the settling of disputes, and the strengthening of communal bonds.

Festival Highlights

Traditional Dances and Music: One of the most captivating aspects of Mwaka Kogwa is the traditional Swahili music and dance performances. Local men and women don vibrant clothing, dance to rhythmic beats, and sing songs that tell stories of their history and aspirations. The energy and passion displayed during these performances are truly infectious.

Mock Fights: A unique and intriguing feature of the festival is the "ngalawa" or "dhow" race. Local men engage in mock fights while balancing on small traditional outrigger canoes. This entertaining spectacle is not only a display of skill but also a representation of the community's ability to resolve conflicts through friendly competition.

Cultural Rituals: Mwaka Kogwa is not just about entertainment; it also involves various rituals that hold deep cultural significance. For example, villagers construct a large bonfire called "kupigania moto" on the first day of the festival. Participants take turns leaping over the fire, symbolizing the cleansing of bad luck and negativity.

Traditional Cuisine: During the festival, visitors have the opportunity to savor authentic Swahili dishes. Local specialties, such as biryani, pilau, and coconut-based sweets, are prepared and shared among the community and guests. It's a chance to indulge in the flavors of Zanzibar's culinary traditions.

Community Bonding: Mwaka Kogwa fosters a sense of togetherness and reconciliation within the community. Disputes are resolved, debts are forgiven, and grievances are put to rest during the festival. This commitment to harmony reflects the festival's underlying message of unity and renewal.

Visiting Mwaka Kogwa Festival

If you're planning to attend the Mwaka Kogwa Festival, it's a good idea to arrange your visit well in advance, as accommodations in Makunduchi Village can fill up quickly during this time. Be prepared to participate in the festivities, engage with locals, and respect their traditions and customs.

Overall, attending the Mwaka Kogwa Festival offers a unique opportunity to witness the living culture of Zanzibar and experience the island's strong sense of community. It's a celebration of heritage, unity, and the enduring spirit of the Swahili people.

Zanzibar Revolution Day

JANUARY 12th, Island-wide with main celebrations in Stone Town

Zanzibar Revolution Day, celebrated on January 12th, is a pivotal event in the history of Zanzibar. This day marks the anniversary of the Zanzibar Revolution, a dramatic political upheaval that occurred in 1964. The revolution led to the overthrow of the Sultanate of Zanzibar, which had ruled the island for centuries, and the establishment of the People's Republic of Zanzibar and Pemba.

The Background: The background to the revolution was a complex interplay of socio-economic, political, and ethnic factors. Zanzibar was a diverse society with a history of tension between the Arab ruling elite and the majority African population. The Arab elite, who controlled most of the wealth and political power, were seen as oppressive by many Africans. Additionally, economic disparities, land issues, and social inequality fueled discontent.

The Revolution: The revolution began on the night of January 12, 1964, when a group of Afro-Shirazi Party (ASP) militants, influenced by leftist and anti-colonial ideologies, launched a coup against the Sultan's regime. The uprising was swift and violent, resulting in the overthrow of Sultan Jamshid bin Abdullah and the execution of several members of the Arab elite.

Establishment of the People's Republic: Following the revolution, the newly formed government, led by ASP leader Abeid Amani Karume, declared the establishment of the People's Republic of Zanzibar and Pemba. The revolution aimed to end the Arab-dominated oligarchy, address social injustices, and promote equality among all ethnic groups.

Celebrations: Zanzibar Revolution Day is observed as a national holiday in Zanzibar, and the main celebrations take place in Stone Town, the historic heart of Zanzibar. The day typically begins with a parade featuring military and civilian participants. There are speeches, cultural performances, and exhibitions highlighting the history of the revolution.

Reflection and Commemoration: This day serves as a time for reflection on the significance of the revolution in shaping the identity and political landscape of Zanzibar. It symbolizes the pursuit of freedom, social justice, and the end of colonial and oppressive rule. The events of January 12, 1964, hold deep historical and cultural importance for the people of Zanzibar, and they are remembered with both solemnity and pride.

Modern Implications: The Zanzibar Revolution significantly altered the political and social dynamics of the island. It paved the way for the merger of Zanzibar with Tanganyika in 1964, forming the United Republic of Tanzania. Today, Zanzibar enjoys a degree of autonomy within the Tanzanian federation and continues to cherish its unique cultural heritage.

Visitors to Zanzibar during Revolution Day can witness the commemorations, engage in discussions about the island's history, and gain insights into the aspirations of its people for a more just and equitable society. It's a day that encapsulates the spirit of Zanzibar's struggle for self-determination and its ongoing journey towards a brighter future.

Zanzibar International Trade Fair (ZITF)

AUGUST, Maisara Grounds, Stone Town

The Zanzibar International Trade Fair, commonly known as ZITF, is a prominent annual event that plays a pivotal role in promoting trade, investment, and economic growth in Zanzibar. This trade fair attracts participants from various sectors, both domestic and international, creating a dynamic platform for business networking, showcasing products and services, and fostering economic partnerships.

History and Significance

The roots of the ZITF date back to the early 1980s when it was first established as an initiative to stimulate economic development on the island. Over the years, it has grown significantly in size and scope, evolving into a highly anticipated event on Zanzibar's calendar. Its primary objectives are to:

Promote Local Industries: ZITF serves as a catalyst for local industries to exhibit their products and innovations, ranging from agriculture and technology to arts and crafts. This exposure helps Zanzibarian businesses expand their reach and connect with potential customers and investors.

Encourage Foreign Investment: The fair attracts foreign investors and businesses interested in exploring opportunities in Zanzibar. It provides a platform for these investors to interact with local counterparts, government officials, and economic stakeholders.

Foster Economic Growth: By showcasing a wide range of goods and services, ZITF contributes to economic diversification and growth in Zanzibar. It plays a crucial role in strengthening the island's economy beyond its traditional sectors.

Event Highlights

ZITF is a multifaceted event that offers a diverse array of activities and exhibits:

Business Exhibition Halls: Various exhibition halls feature products and services from sectors such as agriculture, manufacturing, technology, and tourism.

Visitors can explore the latest innovations and offerings from both local and international exhibitors.

Networking Opportunities: ZITF attracts a broad spectrum of participants, including business leaders, government officials, entrepreneurs, and investors. This diversity creates numerous networking opportunities, facilitating potential collaborations and partnerships.

Seminars and Workshops: The fair often hosts seminars and workshops on topics relevant to Zanzibar's economic development. These sessions provide valuable insights into industry trends, best practices, and investment opportunities.

Cultural Exhibits: Zanzibar's rich cultural heritage is on display through traditional music, dance, and art exhibitions. Visitors can gain a deeper understanding of the island's cultural diversity.

Food and Entertainment: Various food stalls offer a taste of Zanzibar's culinary delights, allowing visitors to sample local dishes and snacks. Additionally, live entertainment performances create a lively and festive atmosphere.

Visitor Experience

For visitors, ZITF is not only an opportunity to engage with the business and economic aspects of Zanzibar but also a chance to experience the island's culture and hospitality. The fair provides a fascinating window into the island's economic aspirations and the vibrancy of its entrepreneurial spirit.

In conclusion, the Zanzibar International Trade Fair (ZITF) stands as a symbol of Zanzibar's commitment to economic growth, diversification, and global integration. It's a must-visit event for anyone interested in understanding the island's economic landscape, forging business connections, and experiencing the convergence of culture and commerce in this enchanting destination.

CHAPTER NINE

PRACTICAL INFORMATION

Let's begin by delving into the essential practical information you need to make the most of your trip to Zanzibar. This section will cover crucial details like currency, time zone, weather, electricity, and communication, ensuring you have a smooth and enjoyable experience on this enchanting island.

Currency Exchange

When visiting Zanzibar, it's essential to be aware of the local currency and the options for currency exchange. The official currency of Zanzibar is the Tanzanian Shilling (TZS). While credit cards are accepted at larger hotels and restaurants, it's wise to carry cash for smaller establishments and local markets.

Currency Exchange Tips

- **Exchange Rates:** Keep an eye on the daily exchange rates to ensure you get a fair deal when exchanging money.
- **ATMs:** Major towns like Stone Town and Nungwi have ATMs where you can withdraw Tanzanian Shillings. Make sure to inform your bank about

your travel plans to avoid any issues with your card.

- **US Dollars:** US dollars are widely accepted and can be used for some payments. It's advisable to carry both Tanzanian Shillings and US dollars.

Time Zone

Zanzibar follows East Africa Time (EAT), which is 3 hours ahead of Coordinated Universal Time (UTC+3). There's no daylight saving time, so the time remains constant throughout the year.

Weather

Zanzibar enjoys a tropical climate with two main seasons - the dry season (June to October) and the wet season (November to April). The best time to visit for pleasant weather is during the dry season when the skies are clear and the temperatures are comfortable. However, even during the wet season, Zanzibar offers a unique charm with lush landscapes and occasional showers.

Electricity

Zanzibar uses a 230V/50Hz electrical system. Most plugs are of the British type with three rectangular prongs. It's advisable to carry a universal adapter if your devices have different plug types.

Communication

Mobile Networks: Zanzibar has good mobile network coverage, and you can easily purchase a local SIM card at the airport or from various shops and vendors. The major mobile service providers are Vodacom, Airtel, and Tigo.

Internet Access: Wi-Fi is widely available in hotels, cafes, and restaurants, especially in tourist areas. However, the quality and speed of the internet may vary. If you need a more stable connection, consider getting a local SIM card with a data package.

Transportation

Local Transport: In Zanzibar, local transport includes daladalas (shared minivans), taxis, and tuk-tuks. Negotiate fares with taxi drivers in advance, and agree on prices for tuk-tuks before setting off. Daladalas are the most budget-friendly option for getting around.

Renting Vehicles: If you plan to explore the island independently, you can rent a car or motorcycle. Ensure you have an international driving permit and drive on the left side of the road.

Ferries and Boats: If you're traveling between Zanzibar and mainland Tanzania, you can take a ferry. The most popular route is from Dar es Salaam to Stone Town. Book tickets in advance during peak seasons.

Wildlife and Conservation

Coral Reefs: Zanzibar boasts magnificent coral reefs, so if you plan to snorkel or dive, remember not to touch or stand on the fragile coral. Practice responsible tourism and avoid disturbing marine life.

Marine Conservation: Many organizations and tour operators in Zanzibar are committed to marine conservation. Consider supporting eco-friendly activities and tours that promote the protection of the ocean's biodiversity.

Travel Insurance

Before your trip, it's highly advisable to purchase comprehensive travel insurance that covers medical emergencies, trip cancellations, and lost or stolen belongings. Ensure your insurance also covers activities like snorkeling and diving if you plan to engage in such adventures.

Local Holidays and Festivals

Zanzibar celebrates various holidays and festivals, some of which may affect your travel plans. Popular celebrations include Eid al-Fitr and Eid al-Adha, which mark the end of Ramadan and the Feast of Sacrifice respectively. During these times, some businesses and services may be closed or operate on limited hours, so plan your visit accordingly.

Respect for the Environment

Zanzibar's natural beauty is a significant attraction, and it's crucial to respect the environment. Avoid littering, dispose of trash responsibly, and choose eco-friendly tour operators and accommodations to support sustainable tourism practices.

Banking and ATM

Zanzibar has several banks and ATMs in major towns and tourist areas. Most banks have ATM machines that accept international credit and debit cards. Credit cards are widely accepted in hotels, larger businesses, and many restaurants. However, having cash on hand is advisable for smaller purchases, street vendors, and in more rural areas where card acceptance may be limited.

Banks in Zanzibar typically operate from Monday to Friday, closing for the weekend. Banking hours are generally from 9:00 AM to 3:00 PM, although this may vary. Plan your currency exchange and banking needs accordingly.

Festival and Event Calendar

Zanzibar hosts various cultural events, music festivals, and religious celebrations throughout the year. Check the local event calendar to see if your visit coincides with any of these vibrant and unique experiences.

Traveler's Health Kit

Consider packing a small traveler's health kit with essentials like over-the-counter medications, insect repellent, sunscreen, and any prescription medications you may need. It's better to be prepared for minor health issues while on your trip.

Tipping

Tipping is customary in Zanzibar, and it's a way to show appreciation for good service. While it's not obligatory, it's generally expected in certain situations. Here are some common tipping guidelines:

- **Restaurants:** If a service charge is not included in the bill, it's customary to leave a tip of 10% to 15% of the total bill.
- **Hotel Staff:** You can tip hotel staff, such as housekeepers and bellboys, a small amount for their services. This is appreciated but not obligatory.
- **Tour Guides and Drivers:** When on guided tours, it's a nice gesture to tip your guide and driver if you were satisfied with their service. The amount can vary based on the length and quality of the tour.

Tipping is a personal choice, so feel free to adjust it based on your experience and level of satisfaction.

Local Laws and Customs

Dress Code: When visiting Stone Town or religious sites like mosques or churches, it's important to dress modestly. For women, this typically means covering shoulders and knees, and for men, it's advisable to avoid wearing shorts in these areas. By respecting the local dress code, you show consideration for the local culture and religious customs.

Photography: Always ask for permission before taking photos of people, especially in rural areas or when capturing personal moments. Some locals may appreciate a small tip for allowing you to photograph them, while others may decline. It's essential to respect their wishes.

Alcohol: Zanzibar is a predominantly Muslim region, and while alcoholic beverages are available, consuming alcohol in public places is discouraged. However, most hotels and resorts have bars where you can enjoy alcoholic drinks.

Drugs: The possession and use of illegal drugs are strictly prohibited in Zanzibar, as they are in Tanzania as a whole. Being caught with illegal substances can result in severe penalties, including imprisonment.

Emergency Contacts

Zanzibar, like any travel destination, prioritizes the safety and well-being of its visitors. It's essential to be aware of the emergency contact information to ensure you can quickly get assistance in case of any unexpected situations during your stay.

1. Police: In Zanzibar, as in many other places, the emergency number for the police is **112**. If you find yourself in a situation where law enforcement assistance is required, dial this number. It's important to note that while Zanzibar is generally safe for tourists, like any location, it's not immune to petty crimes or occasional incidents, so it's wise to be aware of your surroundings and take precautions like securing your belongings.

2. Medical Emergency: In the event of a medical emergency, whether it's a sudden illness, injury, or any health-related concern, you can call **115**. This number will connect you to local medical services and emergency responders. Zanzibar has several hospitals, clinics, and medical facilities, but for serious emergencies, it's recommended to contact this emergency number immediately.

3. Fire Department: While fire incidents are relatively rare in Zanzibar, it's crucial to be prepared. In case of a fire or any fire-related emergency, you can reach the fire department by dialing **114**. Firefighters in Zanzibar are trained to respond to such situations promptly.

4. Tourist Police: Zanzibar also has a specific branch of the police known as the Tourist Police. They are trained to assist tourists and can provide help with issues such as lost passports, travel advice, and other tourist-related concerns. You can typically find Tourist Police stations in tourist areas, including Stone Town and popular beaches. While not an emergency contact, they can be a valuable resource if you need assistance during your trip.

5. Embassies and Consulates: If you're a foreign national and encounter a significant emergency, such as a lost passport, legal issues, or a major crisis, it's advisable to contact your country's embassy or consulate in Dar es Salaam, Tanzania. They can provide consular assistance and guidance in times of need. It's a good idea to have their contact information on hand before you travel.

6. Travel Insurance: It's essential to have comprehensive travel insurance that covers medical emergencies, trip cancellations, and other unforeseen events. Your travel insurance provider will have a 24/7 emergency assistance hotline. Be sure to keep your policy details and emergency contact number readily accessible during your trip.

Having these numbers on hand is crucial for your safety and peace of mind during your travels.

Airport Departure Tax

When departing from Zanzibar, there's an airport departure tax that you'll need to pay in cash, typically in Tanzanian Shillings or US Dollars. Keep some cash on hand to cover this fee, which is subject to change but is usually a modest amount.

Useful Websites and Resources for Your Zanzibar Trip

To ensure a smooth and enjoyable experience, it's essential to have access to the right information and resources. Here, we've compiled a list of useful websites and resources that will be invaluable as you prepare for your Zanzibar adventure.

Zanzibar Tourism website

The official website of Zanzibar's Ministry of Information, Culture, Tourism, and Sports provides up-to-date information on attractions, travel regulations, and events. It's a great starting point for planning your trip.

TripAdvisor website

Travel forums like TripAdvisor offer insights from fellow travelers. You can find recommendations for accommodations, restaurants, and activities, as well as answers to your specific questions.

Booking.com

Booking platforms like Booking.com provide a wide range of accommodation options in Zanzibar. You can read reviews, compare prices, and book hotels, guesthouses, and vacation rentals.

Skyscanner website

Skyscanner is a reliable platform to search for and compare flights to Zanzibar. You can find the best deals and convenient flight options to suit your travel plans.

Google Translate

Google Translate can be especially useful for communicating with locals who may not speak English. Google Translate is a free translation app that allows you to translate text and speech in real-time. It's a great resource for communicating with locals and navigating the island. You can also use the app to take photos of signs or menus and receive instant translations. Download the Greek language pack to access translations offline and communicate with locals more easily.

Google Maps

Google Maps is a useful tool for planning your itinerary in Seychelles, including finding directions, locating restaurants, and exploring the province attractions.

<u>*Where to Get Physical Map*</u>

- **Hotels and Guesthouses:** Many hotels and guesthouses in Zanzibar provide complimentary maps to their guests. If your accommodation

doesn't offer one, you can ask the front desk or concierge if they have maps available or can direct you to a nearby place to purchase one.
- **Tourist Information Centers:** Look for tourist information centers in major towns and tourist hotspots like Stone Town. They typically offer free or low-cost maps and brochures that provide valuable information about the island's attractions and services.

Xe.com

Use currency conversion websites like Xe to check the latest exchange rates for the Tanzanian Shilling (TZS) against your home currency.

Social Media Travel Communities

You can join platforms like Facebook Groups, Reddit, Instagram, etc. media groups and communities dedicated to travel in Zanzibar. Here, you can connect with fellow travelers, ask questions, and share your experiences and recommendations.

Zanzibar Ferry Schedules website

If you prefer traveling by sea, ferries run regularly between Dar es Salaam and Zanzibar. For schedules, ticket booking, and more information you can visit the above website.

These online resources will serve as valuable tools for planning your Zanzibar adventure, ensuring you have access to the latest information and recommendations from both experts and fellow travelers.

CHAPTER TEN

MY MUST- DO LIST FOR AN UNFORGETTABLE EXPERIENCE IN ZANZIBAR

This enchanting island offers a treasure trove of experiences that will leave you with lasting memories. To make the most of your Zanzibar adventure, here is a comprehensive list of 19 must-do activities to create an unforgettable journey through this tropical paradise.

1. Discover the Charms of Stone Town

Begin your Zanzibar adventure in Stone Town, the island's cultural heart. Wander through narrow, winding streets lined with old-world Arab and Swahili architecture. Admire intricately carved wooden doors and discover hidden gems around every corner.

Visit iconic landmarks like the House of Wonders, a palace dating back to the 19th century, and the Palace Museum, which provides insights into Zanzibar's royal history. Explore the Old Fort, originally built by the Portuguese in the 17th century and now hosting cultural events and markets.

Immerse yourself in the local culture by chatting with friendly residents, sampling traditional street food, and observing daily life in the bustling markets. Don't forget to stop by the Darajani Market, where you can find an array of spices, fruits, and fresh seafood.

2. Wander Through Forodhani Gardens

Forodhani Gardens come alive in the evenings with a lively food market. As the sun sets over the Indian Ocean, the gardens transform into a culinary paradise. Sample a variety of local dishes, including Zanzibar pizza, seafood kebabs, and sugar cane juice.

While enjoying your meal, you can often catch street performers, acrobats, and traditional music performances that add to the vibrant atmosphere. It's an excellent place to mingle with both locals and fellow travelers.

3. Relax on Nungwi Beach

Nungwi Beach is renowned for its stunning white sands and crystal-clear waters. Spend your day relaxing on the beach, basking in the tropical sun, and taking refreshing dips in the warm Indian Ocean.

If you're feeling adventurous, consider water sports like snorkeling, diving, or kayaking. Nungwi is also famous for its dhow-building industry, and you can watch skilled craftsmen at work.

4. Explore Kendwa Beach

Kendwa Beach, located just north of Nungwi, offers a more tranquil and less crowded experience. It's ideal for those seeking a peaceful escape and long walks along the shore.

Kendwa Beach is known for its enchanting moonlit beach parties. Join the festivities, dance to local beats, and make friends from around the world. It's a magical way to spend your evenings in Zanzibar.

5. Spice Up Your Day

Zanzibar is famous for its spice plantations, and a guided tour is a sensory delight. You'll learn about the island's history as a spice trading hub and have the chance to smell and taste spices like cloves, vanilla, and cinnamon.

Knowledgeable guides will introduce you to the cultivation of these spices and their uses in traditional Zanzibari cuisine and medicine. It's an educational and aromatic journey that engages all your senses.

6. Encounter Red Colobus Monkeys

Jozani Chwaka Bay National Park is a lush, protected area that's home to the rare and endangered red colobus monkeys. Explore the forested trails, and you might spot these charismatic primates swinging through the trees.

Consider taking a guided tour to learn more about the park's unique biodiversity and conservation efforts. It's a chance to connect with nature and contribute to the preservation of this remarkable species.

7. Dive into the Coral Reefs

Zanzibar boasts some of the world's most pristine coral reefs. Dive beneath the surface to discover a kaleidoscope of marine life, including colorful fish, sea turtles, and vibrant coral formations.

If you're not a certified diver, snorkeling is a fantastic alternative. Many operators offer snorkeling excursions that allow you to explore the shallow reefs and swim alongside a variety of marine species.

8. Set Sail on a Dhow Cruise

Experience the magic of Zanzibar's traditional sailing vessels, dhows, on a memorable cruise. It doesn't matter if you choose a sunset cruise or a full-day adventure, you'll enjoy stunning views of the coastline and the open sea.

Dhows are an integral part of Zanzibari culture and history. On these cruises, you'll often find local sailors sharing stories about their maritime traditions and, in some cases, even inviting you to try your hand at sailing.

9. Savor Zanzibari Cuisine

Zanzibari cuisine is a fusion of Swahili, Indian, and Arabian influences, creating a unique culinary experience. Be sure to sample traditional dishes like biryani, pilau, and the iconic Zanzibar pizza, a delicious street food favorite.

With its abundant seafood, Zanzibar is a seafood lover's paradise. Enjoy the freshest catches of the day, including grilled fish, octopus curry, and lobster, at beachfront restaurants or local eateries.

10. Visit Prison Island

Take a short boat ride to Prison Island, also known as Changuu Island. Initially intended as a prison, the island now offers a historical journey where you can explore the ruins of the old quarantine station and learn about its intriguing past.

The island is also home to a colony of giant Aldabra tortoises. These gentle giants, some over a century old, are fascinating to observe and interact with, making it a unique and educational experience for visitors of all ages.

11. Attend a Taarab Music Show

Zanzibar's cultural heritage is deeply entwined with music, and attending a Taarab music show is an absolute must. Taarab is a blend of African, Arab, and Indian influences, creating enchanting melodies that reflect the island's history. Several venues in Stone Town offer live Taarab performances. Enjoy an evening of soulful music, mesmerizing rhythms, and the melodious voices of local artists. Some shows even include traditional dance performances, adding to the cultural experience.

12. Snorkel with Dolphins

Zanzibar's pristine waters are home to a variety of marine life, including dolphins. Head to Kizimkazi, located on the southern tip of the island, for a chance to swim and snorkel with these playful creatures. Dolphin tours are organized by local guides who know the best spots to find them. The thrill of encountering dolphins in their natural habitat is an unforgettable experience, and the crystal-clear waters of Kizimkazi offer excellent visibility for snorkeling.

13. Wander the Stone Town Markets

Stone Town is a bustling hub of markets and bazaars where you can immerse yourself in the local culture and shop for unique souvenirs. Visit Darajani Market to discover an array of spices, fresh fruits, and local delicacies. The Forodhani Night Market is a culinary delight, with vendors serving up freshly grilled seafood, Zanzibari pizzas, and sweet treats. Don't forget to explore the Mwembeshauru Market for colorful fabrics, intricate jewelry, and handcrafted wooden goods. Bargaining is expected, so hone your negotiation skills and enjoy the lively atmosphere.

14. Discover the Sultan's Palace

Known as Beit al-Sahel, the Sultan's Palace Museum is a historical gem in Stone Town. This museum offers a glimpse into Zanzibar's royal history, showcasing the opulent lifestyle of the sultans who once ruled the island. Explore the beautifully preserved architecture, intricate carvings, and artifacts from the era. The palace's lush gardens are a peaceful escape, providing a serene setting to reflect on Zanzibar's rich heritage.

15. Climb the Old Lighthouse

For panoramic views of Stone Town and the Indian Ocean, venture to the top of the Old Lighthouse (Dhow Countries Music Academy). The climb may be a bit steep, but the reward is worth it. As you ascend, you'll be treated to breathtaking vistas that capture the essence of Zanzibar's beauty. It's an ideal spot for both sunrise and sunset, offering fantastic photo opportunities and a sense of awe as you take in the island's splendor from above.

16. Indulge in a Spa Treatment

Zanzibar is synonymous with relaxation, and what better way to unwind than with a spa day? Many of the island's luxury resorts and hotels offer world-class spa facilities. Surrender to the skilled hands of local therapists and indulge in massages, facials, and body treatments inspired by Zanzibar's traditions and natural resources. The soothing sound of ocean waves and the scent of aromatic spices will enhance your spa experience, leaving you refreshed and rejuvenated.

17. Join a Local Cooking Class

Food is an integral part of Zanzibari culture, and participating in a cooking class is an excellent way to connect with the local way of life. Enroll in a cooking class with experienced Swahili chefs who will guide you through the preparation of traditional dishes. Learn the secrets of Zanzibar's aromatic curries, chapati (flatbread), and sweet treats like mandazi and kashata. It's a hands-on experience that will not only tantalize your taste buds but also allow you to take a piece of Zanzibar's culinary culture home with you.

18. Explore Chumbe Island Coral Park

Chumbe Island Coral Park, a short boat ride from Stone Town, offers a unique opportunity to explore the underwater world of Zanzibar. The park is a protected marine area, known for its stunning coral reefs and diverse marine life. Enjoy snorkeling and guided walks through the pristine forest to learn about the island's conservation efforts. It's a perfect eco-friendly adventure that combines marine conservation with exploration.

19. Attend a Full Moon Party

If your visit to Zanzibar coincides with a full moon, you're in for an unforgettable night. The island comes alive with vibrant full moon parties held on various beaches, particularly in Nungwi and Kendwa. These lively gatherings feature bonfires, drum circles, dancing, and fire shows, creating an electrifying atmosphere. Join the festivities, meet fellow travelers, and dance the night away under the moonlight for an unforgettable island experience.

By checking off these items on your Zanzibar to-do list, you'll immerse yourself in the island's culture, natural beauty, and vibrant atmosphere, ensuring your journey is truly unforgettable. Zanzibar has a way of leaving a lasting impression on all who visit, and these activities will be the highlights of your adventure in this tropical paradise.

CONCLUSION

As we draw the curtains on this comprehensive travel guide to Zanzibar, we hope that your anticipation for this tropical paradise has been stoked and your curiosity piqued. Zanzibar, with its blend of rich history, diverse culture, and breathtaking natural beauty, promises an unforgettable journey for every traveler.

From the historic alleys of Stone Town to the powdery sands of its pristine beaches, Zanzibar unveils its treasures with open arms. The vibrant culture, tantalizing cuisine, and thrilling nightlife provide an immersive experience that will stay with you long after your departure.

Remember to embrace local customs, respect the environment, and tread gently on this delicate island. Whether you're seeking relaxation or adventure, Zanzibar has something to offer every wanderer.

So, pack your bags, secure your visa, and embark on an odyssey to Zanzibar, where azure waters, spice-scented breezes, and warm smiles await. This island of dreams is ready to welcome you to its heart, and with this guide as your companion, you're well-prepared to make the most of your journey.

Zanzibar is more than a destination; it's an experience, a tapestry of colors, flavors, and memories waiting to be woven into your own unique travel story. As you set foot on this tropical gem, may your adventure be filled with wonder, joy, and the spirit of discovery.

As you plan your trip to Zanzibar, keep in mind that this guide is just the beginning. Zanzibar is a dynamic and ever-changing island, with new attractions and experiences popping up all the time. So don't be afraid to explore beyond the pages of this guidebook and discover the island for yourself.

We hope this guide has provided you with the inspiration and information you need to plan an unforgettable trip to Zanzibar. Whether you're visiting for the first time or returning for a repeat visit, we know you will fall in love with this beautiful city and all that it has to offer.

ON A FINAL NOTE

The information provided in this travel guide is intended for general informational purposes as diligent effort has been made to ensure the accuracy of the information provided. Readers are solely responsible for their own travel decisions and activities and should use their judgment when following the suggestions and recommendations provided in this guide. Note that prices, hours of operation, and other details are subject to change without notice. It is always advisable to check with the relevant authorities, businesses, or organizations before making any travel plans or reservations.

The inclusion of any specific product, service, business, or organization in this guide does not constitute an endorsement by the author. Readers are advised to take necessary precautions and follow local laws, regulations, and customs. The author and publisher of this travel guide are not responsible for any inaccuracies or omissions, nor for any damages or losses that may result from following the information provided in this guide.

Thank you for choosing this ZANZIBAR TRAVEL GUIDE, and bon voyage!

PERSONAL NOTES

Printed in Great Britain
by Amazon